ECO 2

Economics for
NCEA Level Two

Anne Younger

NELSON
CENGAGE Learning™

Australia • Brazil • Japan • Korea • Mexico • Singapore • Spain • United Kingdom • United States

NELSON
CENGAGE Learning

Eco2 Economics for NCEA Level Two
1st Edition
Anne Younger

Cover designer: Cheryl Rowe
Text designer: Cheryl Rowe
Cartoon illustrations: Brenda Cantell
Production controller: Siew Han Ong

Any URLs contained in this publication were checked for currency during
the production process. Note, however, that the publisher cannot vouch
for the ongoing currency of URLs.

© 2011 Cengage Learning Australia Pty Limited

For product information and technology assistance,
in Australia call **1300 790 853**;
in New Zealand call **0800 449 725**

For permission to use material from this text or product, please email
aust.permissions@cengage.com

National Library of New Zealand Cataloguing-in-Publication Data
National Library of New Zealand Cataloguing-in-Publication Data

Younger, Anne.
Eco2 / Anne Younger.
ISBN 978-01-7021-571-8
1. Economics. 2. Economics—Problems, exercises, etc.
I. Title.
330.076—dc 22

Cengage Learning Australia
Level 7, 80 Dorcas Street
South Melbourne, Victoria Australia 3205

Cengage Learning New Zealand
Unit 4B Rosedale Office Park
331 Rosedale Road, Albany, North Shore 0632, NZ

For learning solutions, visit **cengage.com.au**

Printed in China by China Translation & Printing Services.
1 2 3 4 5 6 7 15 14 13 12 11

5   Growth

Introduction

1 ▪ Interdependence and the Circular Flow Model

By the end of this unit you will be able to:

- Distinguish between dependence, independence and interdependence.
- Construct a circular flow model of five sectors.
- Identify each sector and flow.
- Differentiate between real and money flows.
- Explain and identify injections and withdrawals.
- Understand that all resources are owned by households and earn a return.
- Explain how changes to one flow or sector will have flow-on effects.

The circular flow model

The **circular flow model**, like all models, simplifies a real life situation. It is designed to give an overview of an entire economy. It is a **macroeconomic** model. Its units represent entire sectors of the economy rather than individual consumers, producers or markets. Each of the five sectors, **households, firms, financial intermediaries, government** and **overseas**, represents the fundamental participating groups in an economy. The **flows** between each of the sectors show the major relationships between the groups. They show the inherent **interdependence** of an economy.

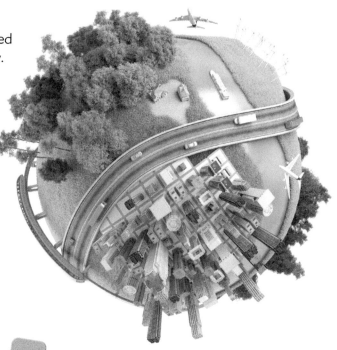

ISBN: 9780170215718

Interdependence

Interdependence is where groups rely upon one another. It is a two-way or mutual reliance. This is a fundamental relationship of economics. It is important to recognise the difference between interdependence, dependence and independence.

Independence
No reliance.
A does not rely on B and B does not rely on A.

Dependence
One-way reliance. B relies on A but A does not rely on B.

Interdependence
Two-way reliance. A relies on B and B relies on A.

The flows

There are two types of flow shown on a circular flow model – **real flows** and **money flows**. It is more usual to have only the money flows shown. An underlying assumption of the model is that households own all resources. When they are used in production, households are paid for their use. Economically speaking, all resources (factors of production) earn an **income** or **return**.

Money flows ⟶ are financial movements between sectors. As the name suggests they are flows of money, for example households paying for the goods and services they purchase from firms.

Real flows ⟶ are movements of goods and services or resources between sectors. Examples include the actual goods and services households buy from firms or the goods and services firms export overseas.

The two-sector model

The two essential participants of any economy are consumers (users of goods and services) and producers (makers of goods and services). In the model all consumers are grouped together and called **households**. All producers are grouped as **firms**. People are classified by what they are doing. A person can be both a consumer and a producer but the function of production is attributed to firms and the function of consumption to households. While all people are consumers, not all people are producers.

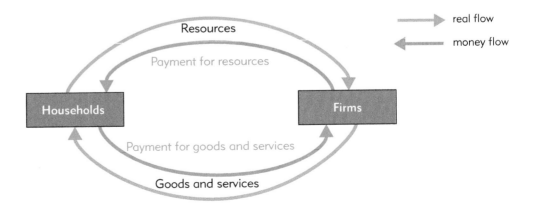

ISBN: 9780170215718

Although an underlying assumption of the model is that the households own all resources, this is contrary to how the economy may look. Generally we tend to think of the resources being owned and controlled by the firms. It is not difficult to reconcile our view of the world with the model. Remember, ultimately households own all firms and thus households must also own all resources.

The households allow firms to use the resources (real flow) and in return are paid an income for this use (money flow). Households use this income to pay (money flow) for goods and services (real flow) they buy from firms. These goods and services satisfy the households' wants. **Firms and households are interdependent.**

There are specific terms used to identify the returns to each of the factors of production. They are shown below:

Resources	Factors of Production	Return
Natural ⟶	⟶ Land	Rent
Man-made ⟶	⟶ Capital	Interest
Human	⟶ Labour	Wages
	⟶ Entrepreneurship	Profit

It is important to be aware of the differences and to use the terms appropriately.

The two-sector model on page 6 represents a very basic economy. The addition of further sectors is more representative of a modern economy.

The three-sector model

Not all income is spent; households save some income with the financial sector. The financial sector provides an opportunity for households to save and for firms to access these savings by borrowing these funds for investment.

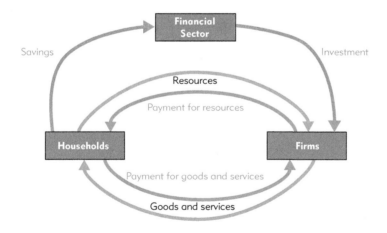

Just as 'capital' has a specific, narrow definition in economics, so too do 'savings' and 'investment'.

Savings   This is income not spent, or forgoing consumption now for consumption later. Households save.

Investment Investment is an increase in capital or man-made resources. Firms invest.

ISBN: 9780170215718

The four-sector model

Another major participant in an economy is the government. Essentially governments collect taxes and then either redistribute income (take from one group and give to another) or spend on defence, health, education and law and order. The money they are spending is collected in taxes. The redistribution of income takes income from one group of households (for example, the employed), and transfers it to less economically strong households through welfare benefits.

The term **transfer payment** indicates a one-way payment with nothing expected in return. Examples of transfer payments include welfare payments such as the unemployment benefit, domestic purposes benefit, sickness benefit and subsidies, which are payments to producers to help lower their costs of production.

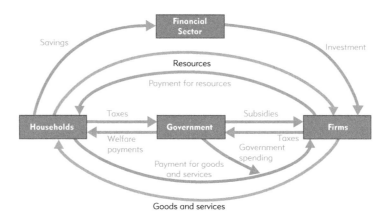

The five-sector model

The model depicted above shows a closed economy in the sense that it is closed off from the international economy. There is no interaction with overseas economies. The final sector to be added is the overseas sector.

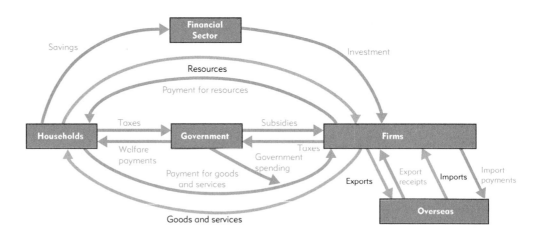

The real flows associated with the overseas sector are:

1 The goods and services that are sold by New Zealand to overseas countries — EXPORTS.

2 The goods and services that are bought by New Zealand from overseas countries — IMPORTS.

ISBN: 9780170215718

The money flows are the payments associated with the import and export of goods. The payments for goods and services bought overseas are called **import payments** and the payments made by overseas countries for our goods and services are called **export receipts**.

Injections and withdrawals

The central relationship shown by the money flows between households and firms is the 'circle' of the circular flow. This flow is shown below.

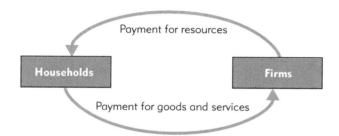

An injection is a money flow into this central 'circle' flow. Injections cause the central circle flow to expand. **This is an increase in economic activity.** The injections are listed in the table.

The injections are printed green on the diagram below.

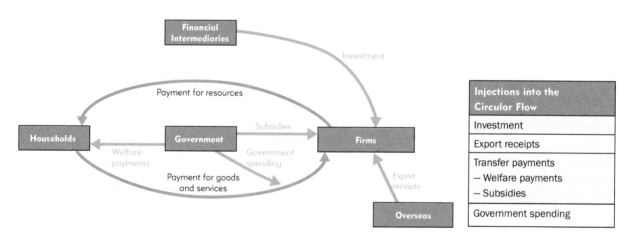

Injections into the Circular Flow
Investment
Export receipts
Transfer payments — Welfare payments — Subsidies
Government spending

A withdrawal is a money flow out of the central 'circle' flow. Withdrawals cause the central circle flow to contract. **This is a decrease in economic activity.** The withdrawals are listed in the table.

The withdrawals are printed green on the diagram below.

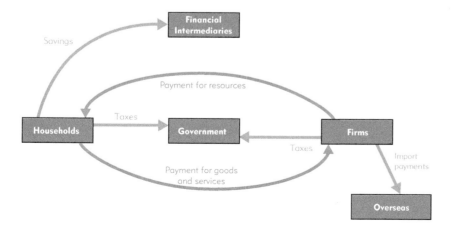

Withdrawals from the Circular Flow
Savings
Import payments
Taxes — Income tax — Company tax

ISBN: 9780170215718

1 Match the terms in Column A with the correct definition in Column B.

Column A
1 money flow
2 rent
3 profit
4 investment
5 households
6 circular flow model
7 export receipts
8 interdependence
9 withdrawal

Column B
a the sector in the circular flow model representing consumers
b a diagram representing the major relationships within an economy
c the income earned by households for the factor of production — the entrepreneur
d payments received for selling goods and services overseas
e two-way or mutual reliance
f an increase in man-made resources
g a money flow away from the central circular flow
h a financial movement between sectors
i the income earned by households for the factor of production — land

2 Copy and complete the table below.

Resources	Factors of Production	Return	Example
	Capital		
		Rent	
Man-made			
Human			Doctor
		Profit	
	Land		
	Labour		

3 Copy and complete this diagram by labelling all flows and sectors.

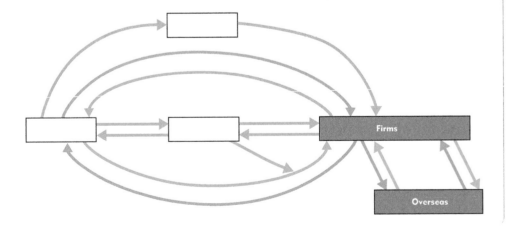

ISBN: 9780170215718

4 For each of these situations, identify the appropriate money flows in the circular flow model.

Situation
a The government buys new textbooks for state schools
b Households buy garden supplies
c Cars are imported from Japan
d Firms borrow to buy machinery
e Households forgo current consumption
f Butter is sent to France
g Welfare benefits are reduced

5 Define these terms:
- Investment
- Profit
- Wages
- Rent
- Financial intermediaries
- Consumption expenditure
- Export receipts
- Import payments
- Withdrawals
- Injections

6 Explain the effect of an increased injection into the circular flow.

7 Explain the effect of an increased withdrawal from the circular flow.

8 Copy and complete the table below. The first has been done for you as an example.

Scenario	Represented by...	Which affects...	Which will have a flow-on effect to ...
Increased exports to Japan	Export receipts	Firms	• Household incomes increase • Taxes increase
Household spending falls			
Government reduces company tax			
Imports fall			

ISBN: 9780170215718

Economics for NCEA Level 2

2 ■ The Production Possibility Frontier Model

By the end of this unit you will be able to:

- Explain and construct a Production Possibility Frontier.
- Outline the meaning of different output combinations and relate these to resource use.
- Illustrate changes in resources and technology on the Production Possibility Frontier.

The Production Possibility model

The **Production Possibility Frontier model** is an economic model that shows an economy's potential output. It is a **static model**. This means it shows a picture of the economy at a given time. Any changes to this are shown as a before and an after picture.

The model has **two assumptions**. Each frontier is drawn for a **given or fixed amount of resources** and **a given or fixed level of technology**. The Production Possibility Frontier model can be used to illustrate a number of economic concepts, particularly those related to growth.

The model shows the maximum output combinations possible with **given resources** and **given technology**. This means that for a fixed amount of resources and technology (the methods used to produce goods and services) there is a physical limit on output.

Constructing a Production Possibility Frontier

The Production Possibility Schedule shows, with its given resources and technology, the various output choices available to the economy of Mansuria. Notice we have assumed only two products can be produced.

Mansuria can produce:
- 100 weapons and no food
OR
- 99 weapons and 1 food
OR
- 96 weapons and 2 food
OR
- 91 weapons and 3 food
OR
- 84 weapons and 4 food
OR
- 75 weapons and 5 food
OR
- 64 weapons and 6 food
OR
- 51 weapons and 7 food
OR
- 36 weapons and 8 food
OR
- 19 weapons and 9 food
OR
- no weapons and 10 food

Production Possibility Schedule for Mansuria	
Weapons (number per week)	**Food** (tonnes per week)
100	0
99	1
96	2
91	3
84	4
75	5
64	6
51	7
36	8
19	9
0	10

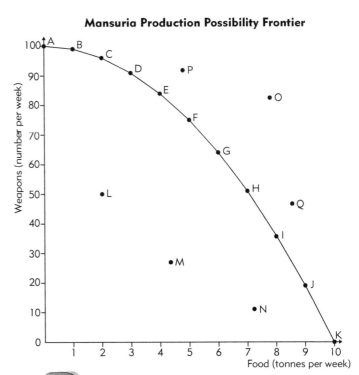

Mansuria Production Possibility Frontier

ISBN: 9780170215718

The model is generally shown as a graph where the two goods (or two bundles of goods) are shown on the two axes. It is also commonly referred to by its acronym (PPF). Production Possibility Frontiers can also be called Production Possibility Curves (PPC).

Points on the Production Possibility Frontier

The frontier (page 12) maps out the maximum output combinations the economy can possibly produce. It shows the productive capacity or potential of the economy. The actual combination the economy operates at is shown as a point.

Any point along the frontier (points A, B, C, D, E, F, G, H, I, J, K) shows an economy operating at its productive capacity. It is fully utilising all of its resources and technology.

If an economy is operating within the frontier (points L, M, N) then it is operating below its potential. There are underutilised resources or technology. Resources and/or technology that could be used to make goods and services are not currently being used. They are idle.

Any point outside of the frontier (points O, P, Q) is unattainable with the given (current) level of resources or technology.

Opportunity cost and the Production Possibility Frontier

If an economy changes its output combination, then there will be an opportunity cost of that choice. This opportunity cost can be shown on the PPF graph.

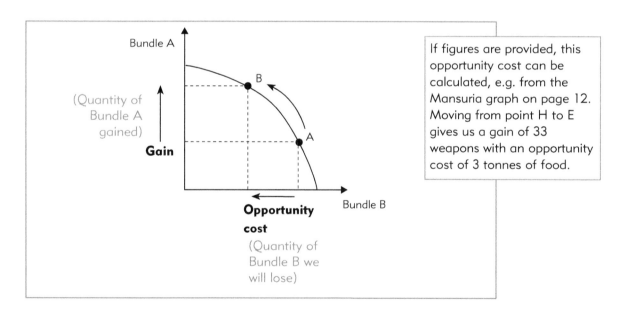

Bundle A

(Quantity of Bundle A gained)

Gain

B

A

Opportunity cost
(Quantity of Bundle B we will lose)

Bundle B

If figures are provided, this opportunity cost can be calculated, e.g. from the Mansuria graph on page 12. Moving from point H to E gives us a gain of 33 weapons with an opportunity cost of 3 tonnes of food.

Shifts of the Production Possibility Frontier

Points outside of the frontier are currently unattainable because of the current limit on resources and technology. If an economy is able to secure additional resources by, for example, discovering new natural resources (e.g. oil), making more man-made resources or improving technology (e.g. applying new scientific knowledge to the production process), then the possible output combinations will have increased and a new frontier is drawn. This is described as a shift outwards of the PPF.

ISBN: 9780170215718

Examples are shown below:

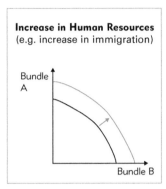

Increase in Human Resources
(e.g. increase in immigration)

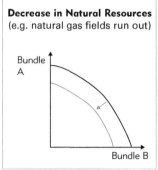

Decrease in Natural Resources
(e.g. natural gas fields run out)

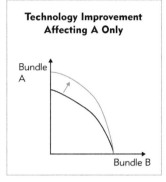

Technology Improvement Affecting A Only

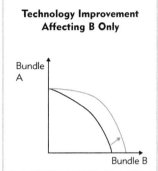

Technology Improvement Affecting B Only

Human Resources

Technology

Natural Resources

ACTIVITY

1 Construct a Production Possibility Frontier for Gustavia using the Production Possiblity Schedule given below. Put butter on the vertical axis.

The Production Possibility Schedule for Gustavia	
Butter (000 kg)	Tractors (00)
0	105
10	100
20	90
30	75
40	55
50	30
60	0

On your graph, label the following points:

a Point A, where there are idle resources.

b Point B, which is unattainable with current resources.

c Point C, where Gustavia is specialising in the production of tractors.

d Point D, where Gustavia is specialising in the production of butter.

e Points E and F, where there is full utilisation of resources and technology and both goods are being produced.

f Illustrate the opportunity cost of moving from 75 tractors to 90 tractors.

ISBN: 9780170215718

2 For each of the diagrams suggest a reason for the change in the PPF shown.

a

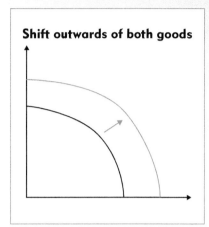

Shift outwards of both goods

b

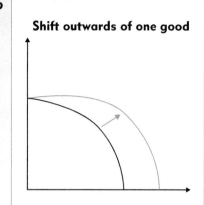

Shift outwards of one good

c

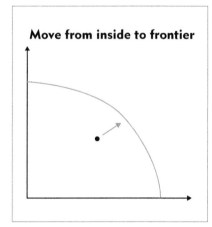

Move from inside to frontier

d

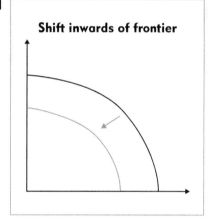

Shift inwards of frontier

3 Draw PPFs to illustrate each of the following statements.
   a New Zealand discovers oil off the Kapiti Coast.
   b Australia exhausts its bauxite deposits.
   c The New Zealand unemployment rate is halved.
   d New Zealand enters a recession.
   e Economic downturn sees factories mothballed.
   f Huge government investment in new infrastructure.
   g Hydro-electricity shortages due to low lake levels.
   h Major immigration into New Zealand.

ISBN: 9780170215718

Inflation

1 ▪ Inflation: Defining the Issue

By the end of this unit you will be able to:

- Explain the difference between a persistent rise in the general level of prices and a price rise in a particular market.
- Define and distinguish between inflation, deflation and disinflation.

Inflation, deflation and disinflation

Inflation is a rise in the general level of prices. Inflation is not a rise in the price of one good or even many goods but rather an increase in the overall level of prices.

In a period of inflation there will be goods that have fallen in price, goods that have not changed in price, and goods that have risen in price. For it to be considered inflation the overall level of prices has to rise. So, a rise in the price of lollies since your parents were young is not in itself inflation but as nearly every good — groceries, petrol, clothing — has risen in price since your parents were young, we would say that this is iinflation.

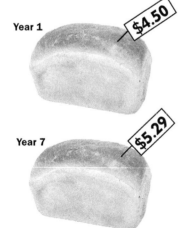

Year 1 $4.50

Year 7 $5.29

Deflation is a fall in the general level of prices. A third term, **disinflation**, refers to a fall in the rate of inflation, or the general level of prices is rising but rising more slowly than previously. Disinflation is a special type of inflation.

To avoid any confusion over the price of one good versus the general level of prices let's simplify the situation. This practice of simplifying the situation is common in economics. Simplifications are also called **assumptions**.

In our simplified world we are looking at an economy with bread as its only good. We will look at the effect of changes in the price of bread. As we are looking at this economy's entire range of goods we can be sure we are looking at inflation, deflation and disinflation rather than simply price changes of individual goods.

ISBN: 9780170215718

Year	Price of bread (loaf)	Change in the price of bread ($/loaf)	Change in the price of bread (%)	Explanation
Year 1	$4.50		–	With no prior data to compare to, the % change cannot be calculated
Year 2	$4.79	$0.29	6.4%	The price of our bread has risen — INFLATION
Year 3	$4.96	$0.17	3.5%	Again the price of bread has risen BUT the rise is smaller than the last rise — DISINFLATION
Year 4	$5.36	$0.40	8.1%	Prices have risen and by more than the last measure — INFLATION
Year 5	$5.17	($0.19)	–3.5%	Prices have fallen — DEFLATION
Year 6	$5.04	($0.13)	–2.5%	Prices have fallen — DEFLATION
Year 7	$5.29	$0.25	5.0%	Prices have risen and they were not rising before — INFLATION

Remember your percentage change formula:

$$\frac{\text{difference}}{\text{original}} \times 100$$

Example: Year 3

$$4.96 - 4.79 = 0.17$$

$$\frac{0.17}{4.79} \times \frac{100}{1} = 3.5\%$$

This same information could be shown graphically.

Year	Change in the price of bread (%)
Year 1	–
Year 2	6.4%
Year 3	3.5%
Year 4	8.1%
Year 5	–3.5%
Year 6	–2.5%
Year 7	5.0%

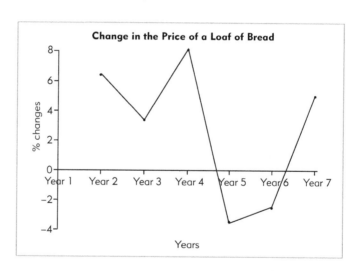

Although percentage and dollar amount changes are shown in the table, the percentage changes are more useful for analysis. Depending on the starting value, the dollar change may or may not be significant. A $1million price rise sounds huge but if the product was worth $100 million, then the price rise is not as significant. The percentage change figure of 1% increase gives a clearer picture of proportionate changes.

Price Rise $1 million = 1%

$100 million

ISBN: 9780170215718

Economics for NCEA Level 2

1 Define the following three terms:
   a Inflation
   b Deflation
   c Disinflation

2 Using the percentage changes shown in the table at right, state the years in which there has been INFLATION, DISINFLATION or DEFLATION.

Year	% Change in General Price Level
1	3.2%
2	2.5%
3	4.1%
4	−3.6%
5	−2.4%
6	0%

3 For each of the years given in the table at right:
   a Identify the change in the price of Good A in dollars.
   b Identify the percentage change in the price of Good A.
   c State whether there has been INFLATION, DISINFLATION and DEFLATION.

Year	Price of Good A
Year 1	$12.50
Year 2	$15.00
Year 3	$16.00
Year 4	$11.00
Year 5	$12.00

4 Identify whether the following statements are true (T), false (F) or unable to be determined (U) using the graph below.
   a Prices rose over all of the years shown.
   b Deflation occurs in the year ending December 2013.
   c There is no overall price increase in the year ending December 2012.
   d The price for each individual good/service rose by 5% in 2014.
   e The highest rate of inflation occurred in 2014.
   f The inflation rate was higher in the year ending December 2011 than in the year ending December 2010.
   g There was an overall fall in prices in the year ending December 2013.
   h Disinflation occurred in only one year.

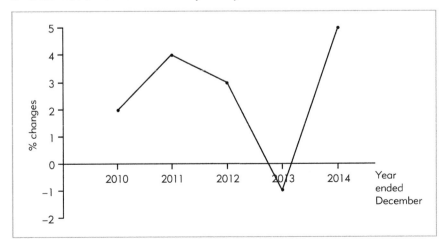

ISBN: 9780170215718

5 From the grah below, identify the period in which:
  a INFLATION occurred.
  b DISINFLATION occurred.
  c DEFLATION occurred.
  d There was no INFLATION.
  e Prices increased.
  f Prices fell.
  g The rate of inflation fell.

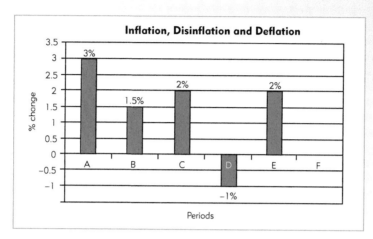

6 For each of the following statements identify whether the statement is describing INFLATION, DISINFLATION, DEFLATION or none of these phenomena:
  a The price of apples has risen sharply as growers experience difficult weather prior to harvesting crops.
  b Although prices have not risen as sharply as in previous years, consumers are showing a reluctance to purchase.
  c Prices have shown a slight drop this year following increased Middle East stability and steadily falling global oil prices.
  d Price rises remain steady.

7 Explain the difference between the following pairs of terms:
  a Inflation and deflation
  b Inflation and disinflation
  c Deflation and disinflation

8 Explain why an increase in bus fares is not inflation but an increase in the price of oil may be inflation.

ISBN: 9780170215718

2 ▪ Measuring Inflation Using Price Indexes

By the end of this unit you will be able to:

- Explain index numbers.
- Explain how inflation is measured.

The concept of a **general level of prices** is crucial to the concept of inflation. One measure incorporating all the individual prices needs to be established. **Vastly different prices** have to be accommodated. The price of a bar of soap and the price of a house need to be measured in the same survey. The **prices of a full range of different goods** in the economy must be collected again and again so that price changes can be measured. You saw previously that the actual price level is not as important in determining inflation as percentage changes. The key point is the **degree of change** — *did prices change and by how much?* **Index numbers** are a useful mathematical tool to use for this.

Index numbers

An index number shows the percentage change from a given starting point. The starting point is called the **base**. The base number is given the value of 1000 (or sometimes 100).

Using the example from the previous unit of a loaf of bread, our index numbers would have been:

Year	Price of bread (loaf)	Change in the price of a loaf of bread from Year 1 ($)	Change in the price of a loaf of bread from Year 1 (%)	Index Number Base = Year 1
Year 1	$4.50		–	1000 (base number)
Year 2	$4.79	$0.29	6.4%	1064 (1000 + % change)
Year 3	$4.96	$0.46	10.2%	1102 (1000 + % change)
Year 4	$5.36	$0.86	19.1%	1191 (1000 + % change)
Year 5	$5.17	$0.67	14.9%	1149 (1000 + % change)
Year 6	$5.04	$0.54	12.0%	1120 (1000 + % change)
Year 7	$5.29	$0.79	17.6%	1176 (1000 + % change)

The difference between a base number of 100 and 1000 is one of accuracy. Although we do not show the decimal place, 1000 actually means 100.0. You must remember the decimal place is there so that you line up your columns correctly when adding. For instance: 1000 + 6.4 does not equal 1006.4 because 1000 is actually 100.0 so 100.0 + 6.4 = 106.4 and we then drop the decimal place again to get 1064 as shown in the table.

The numbers in this table differ from the ones in the previous unit, where the calculation of percentage change was from one year to the next. In this calculation the percentage change is from any one year back to the base year.

While the table is designed to show you the meaning of an index number, there is a quicker way of calculating the index numbers.

ISBN: 9780170215718

Year	Price of bread	Index Number Base = Year 1
Year 1	$4.50	1000 (base number)
Year 2	$4.79	1064 (4.79/4.50 x 1000)
Year 3	$4.96	1102 (4.96/4.50 x 1000)
Year 4	$5.36	1191 (5.36/4.50 x 1000)
Year 5	$5.17	1149 (5.17/4.50 x 1000)
Year 6	$5.04	1120 (5.04/4.50 x 1000)
Year 7	$5.29	1176 (5.29/4.50 x 1000)

Formula:

$$\frac{\text{new price}}{\text{base price}} \ \ x \ \ \frac{\text{base number}}{1}$$

Interpreting a set of index numbers is easy. We know from our construction of this set of index numbers that they show the percentage changes from the base year. So, there was a 6.4% increase in the price of bread between Year 1 and Year 2: 1064 – 1000 = 64 (but don't forget the invisible decimal place, so we get 6.4%). Similarly from between Years 1 and 6 the price of a loaf of bread rose by 12.0%, and between Years 1 and 7, by 17.6%.

Year	Index Number Base = Year 1
Year 1	1000
Year 2	1064
Year 3	1102
Year 4	1191
Year 5	1149
Year 6	1120
Year 7	1176

If we want to know how much the price of bread rose between two non-base years, then we must use our percentage change formula. For Years 4 and 5:

$$\frac{(1149 - 1191)}{1191} \ \ X \ \ 100 \ \ = \ \ -3.5\%$$

Compare this figure with the one calculated in the previous unit on page 17.

ACTIVITY

1 Calculate the annual inflation rates for 2009 and 2010 using the index numbers provided in the table below.

Year	Price Index
2008	1078
2009	1085
2010	1096

2 Calculate the annual inflation rates for 2011 and 2012 using the index numbers provided in the table below.

Year	Price Index
2010	1258
2011	1356
2012	1378

3 Calculate the annual inflation rates for Year Y and Year Z using the index numbers provided in the table below.

Year	Price Index
X	1032
Y	1056
Z	1028

ISBN: 9780170215718

Economics for NCEA Level 2

ACTIVITY

4 Copy the table below. Calculate the percentage changes and use them to develop one index with a base of 100 and another with a base of 1000. Year 1 is the base year.

Year	Data ($)	Percentage change (from base year)	Index One Base Year 1 = 100	Index Two Base Year 1 = 1000
1	46.90	–	100	1000
2	54.80			
3	63.59			
4	72.00			
5	78.00			

5

Year	Index One	Index Two
2008	104	1044
2009	106	1061
2010	107	1073
2011	107	1072
2012	108	1076
2013	108	1084

a Calculate the rate of inflation for each of the years shown using Index One.

b Calculate the rate of inflation for each of the years shown using Index Two.

c Explain how Index One differs from Index Two.

d Identify the best index and justify your choice.

Throughout the previous discussion we have been using the simplification of a one-good economy. This is not a very likely scenario. The general level of prices of any economy must measure the price changes of all goods.

ISBN: 9780170215718

3 ▪ The Consumer Price Index

By the end of this unit you will be able to:

- Explain what the Consumer Price Index (CPI) is.
- Explain how the Consumer Price Index (CPI) is constructed.
- Interpret and analyse the limitations of the Consumer Price Index (CPI).
- Identify other measures of inflation such as PPI, CGPI and FEPI.

The **Consumer Price Index (CPI)** is a **weighted price index.** It is used to measure changes in the general price level for goods purchased by the average New Zealand household. When including more than one good's price change in the calculation, it is possible to weight the price changes. This means taking greater account of some price changes than others. If households spend more on one good than others, this good is weighted more heavily. Its price changes are given greater significance in our calculation of the overall combined price effects. The weightings used in the CPI are taken from the Household Economic Survey. This is a *Statistics New Zealand* survey that collects data on the spending habits of New Zealanders. The CPI is the most commonly used and the **official measure** of inflation in New Zealand.

The basket of goods

The prices of over 700 individual items are surveyed for the CPI. These goods are organised into eleven groups. Box 1 shows the weightings given to each group:

Box 1	CATEGORY WEIGHTS		
	June 2002 quarter	June 2006 quarter	June 2008 quarter
Group	Percent [1]		
Food	17.21	17.38	17.83
Alcoholic beverages and tobacco	8.72	7.20	6.76
Clothing and footwear	4.77	4.75	4.48
Housing and household utilities	21.52	20.02	22.75
Household contents and services	5.13	5.49	5.26
Health	4.83	5.23	5.09
Transport	15.51	17.24	16.18
Communication	2.92	3.26	3.21
Recreation and culture	9.73	10.21	9.54
Education	1.65	2.08	1.78
Miscellaneous goods and services	8.01	7.13	7.12
All groups	**100.00**	**100.00**	**100.00**

[1] Percentages may not sum to totals due to rounding.

Source: *Statistics NZ*

ISBN: 9780170215718

Economics for NCEA Level 2

These groups are then divided into 21 subgroups and then 73 sections. This detail allows a greater degree of analysis of where inflationary or deflationary pressures are coming from.

ACTIVITY

1 a Classify the following items using the groups given in Box 1 on the previous page: pork, wine, personal care, communication equipment and services, men's footwear, refuse charges, motor vehicle running and maintenance, air travel, sweets, crisps and nuts, furniture, energy, medical and health supplies, margarine, sunscreen cream, herbal teas, petrol, movie tickets, DVD rental fees, umbrellas.

b Explain the term weighted.

c Explain why it is important to weight a price index.

2

In the June 2011 quarter compared with the March 2011 quarter:
- The consumer price index (CPI) rose 1.0 percent.
- The main upward contribution came from transport (up 2.7 percent), reflecting higher prices for petrol and airfares.
- Food prices rose 1.1 percent, with higher prices for grocery food and vegetables.
- Housing and household utility prices rose 0.9 percent, with higher prices for electricity.

Source: *Statistics NZ*

a Explain how the subgroups can add greater detail on where individual price changes are impacting on the general price level.

b Although a price rise in a single market is not inflation explain how these can lead to inflation.

Collecting reliable and consistent data is important. Price changes are not always obvious. Sometimes the size of a good changes but the price doesn't. In effect this is a price change and *Statistics New Zealand* adjusts its figures accordingly. The CPI endeavours to take account of quality changes that are coupled with price changes.

Statistics New Zealand tries to price an item where New Zealand households most commonly purchase it. For instance, if we most likely buy our milk from a dairy, then the price of milk is weighted more heavily in favour of dairies. Recent **outlet** changes incorporated into the CPI include alcohol prices from supermarkets and direct mail prices.

ISBN: 9780170215718

ISBN: Inflation

The population weightings

Prices are surveyed across 15 urban areas. These areas are then weighted according to the number of New Zealand households in each area. Any price changes that occur in less densely populated areas affect fewer people than price changes in more densely populated areas. The price changes are weighted according to the number of people likely to be affected.

Box 2			
	1993	2006	2008
Whangarei	4.11	3.63	3.64
Auckland	28.39	32.63	32.98
Hamilton	6.44	9.39	9.93
Tauranga	4.19	4.42	4.45
Rotorua	4.68	1.94	1.88
Napier-Hastings	5.54	4.74	4.69
New Plymouth	3.16	2.56	2.54
Whanganui	1.97	1.59	1.526
Palmerston North	4.60	3.93	3.86
Wellington	11.99	11.23	11.13
Christchurch	11.48	11.46	11.55
Timaru	2.11	1.38	1.39
Nelson	3.37	4.04	3.95
Dunedin	4.82	4.80	4.77
Invercargill	3.15	2.27	2.20
Total	**100.00**	**100.00**	**100.00**

Source: *Statistics NZ*

CPI revisions

The CPI is reviewed regularly. Generally the revisions have occurred every five years, but recently the cycle has been shortened to three years. As the CPI needs to reflect current spending, it is necessary to ensure that the survey changes with changes in New Zealanders' spending habits. The 2008 review saw, for example, fresh pineapples replace fresh peaches, and the addition of housekeeping services, heat pumps, hummus dip and cooked chickens priced at supermarkets. This reflects increased expenditure on these products by New Zealanders. The 2008 review also saw the following items removed from the basket: calculators, CRT television sets, saveloys, rose bushes and writing paper (to be replaced by computer printer paper).

Limitations of the CPI

Remember that many statistics are based on **sampling** — a representative sample of the whole is used to *approximate* the whole. This does not mean they are meaningless. The CPI is generally regarded as an internationally comparable statistic and a fair representation of inflation in New Zealand. However it is important to recognise its limitations:

1   The rate of inflation calculated by the CPI is unlikely to be the actual rate of inflation experienced by any real individual or household because it is an average.

ISBN: 9780170215718

2 The CPI is reviewed every three years and so is unlikely to match current expenditure patterns, especially towards the end of the three-year period. Problems include:
   • new products, e.g. Internet charges were not included until 1999
   • products that change in popularity or usage.

3 It can be difficult to allow for changes in the quality of products over time, e.g. cars.

4 Goods that are too difficult to gather reliable and consistent price information on are not included. This includes secondhand goods.

5 While accepted as an internationally comparable statistic, be aware that there are possible discrepancies such as overseas weightings and review periods. Baskets may not be comparable across different countries.

ACTIVITY

1 Explain why each of the people described below is unlikely to experience the rate of inflation given by the CPI.

   a A vegan.
   b A person living in rural New Zealand.
   c A student living at a boarding house with 25 other students.
   d A shopper who buys exclusively from the Internet.
   e An enthusiast who buys goods secondhand at auction to repair and do up.
   f A single person with a mortgage-free home living on a very high income.

2 a

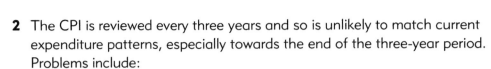

CPI now includes e-books and iPads

In a sign of the changing times, tablet computers, e-books and digital movie downloads have been added to the consumer price index, while dictionaries and envelopes drop out.   2011

Explain why it is necessary to review the basket of goods used in the CPI every three years.

   b

We are eating out in restaurants less. Takeaways, on the other hand, are up.   2011

Explain why the CPI weightings on outlets would have to be altered in light of these changes in consumer behaviour.

Reading the CPI statistics

The CPI statistics are published quarterly. Inflation statistics are often presented as a rate of inflation compared to the previous quarter, i.e. the percentage change from one quarter to the next (see column 4 of the table on the next page). What is not readily accessible from the index numbers is the ANNUAL rate of inflation. One way of coming to an annual figure is to calculate the percentage change between a quarterly figure and the same quarterly figure from a year ago. A sample of recent figures is shown on the next page.

Consumer Price Index Base: June 2006 quarter (= 1000)			
Quarterly	2006	Index Base = June 2006 Quarter	Inflation Rate
2003	Mar	913	2.5
	Jun	913	1.5
	Sep	918	1.5
	Dec	924	1.6
2004	Mar	928	1.5
	Jun	935	2.4
	Sep	941	2.5
	Dec	949	2.7
2005	Mar	953	2.8
	Jun	962	2.8
	Sep	973	3.4
	Dec	979	3.2
2006	Mar	985	3.3
	Jun	1000	4.0
	Sep	1007	3.5
	Dec	1005	2.6
2007	Mar	1010	2.5
	Jun	1020	2.0
	Sep	1025	1.8
	Dec	1037	3.2
2008	Mar	1044	3.4
	Jun	1061	4.0
	Sep	1077	5.1
	Dec	1072	3.4
2009	Mar	1075	3.0
	Jun	1081	1.9
	Sep	1095	1.7
	Dec	1093	2.0
2010	Mar	1097	2.0
	Jun	1099	1.7
	Sep	1111	1.5
	Dec	1137	4.0
2011	Mar	1146	4.5
	Jun	1157	5.3

Source: *Statistics NZ*

Other measures of inflation

While the CPI is the most common price index, there are others that look at a different range of goods and are thus more useful in certain contexts. These indexes include:

- **PPI** Producers Price Index: Measures the changes in the general level of prices for the productive sector, e.g. goods and services sampled include materials, fuels and electricity.
- **CGPI** Capital Goods Price Index: Measures the price changes of capital assets bought by producers, e.g. goods sampled include ovens and furnace burners, office and accounting machinery.
- **FEPI** Farm Expenses Price Index: Measures the change in input costs for the New Zealand farming industry, e.g. input costs sampled include fertiliser, weed and pest control.

ISBN: 9780170215718

ACTIVITY

Below is a line graph of the data on page 27 (column 4). Identify periods of:

a inflation

b deflation

c disinflation.

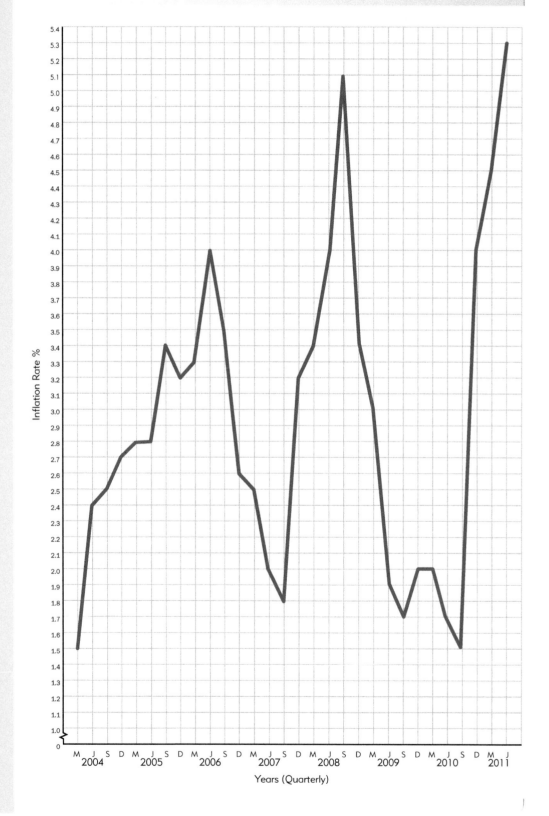

ISBN: 9780170215718

4 ▪ An Economic Model of Inflation: The Quantity Theory of Money

By the end of this unit you will be able to:

- Explain the concept of money, its functions and characteristics.
- Explain the theoretical link between money and prices.
- Explain the Quantity Theory of Money.
- Explain the business cycle.
- Explain the relationship between the Quantity Theory of Money and the business cycle.

What is money?

'Money is what money does.' Essentially, what we know as money can be made out of anything. What we use as money — shells, cows, notes or electronic numbers — is not important. What is important is what money does. Money has four functions:

1 Medium of exchange
2 Standard of value
3 Store of value
4 Means of deferred payment.

The most important of these is *money as a medium of exchange.* This function allows people to abandon barter as a means of exchange. Instead of having to swap (barter) a good or service for another good or service, money acts as the go-between. We swap our labour for money and then use the money to buy goods and services. In order to be used as a medium of exchange money must have the following characteristics:

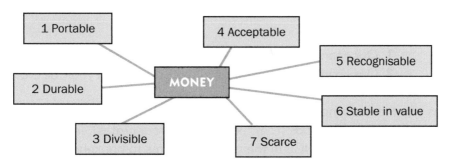

In New Zealand our money, our legal tender, is made up of notes and coins. Notes and coins must be accepted, by law, in return for goods and services. Many other forms of money are also accepted, e.g. cheques, EFTPOS, and telephone and Internet banking, but they *do not have to be* by law.

Legal Tender

1 There are limits to the amount that must be accepted in the form of coins in New Zealand.

2 Credit cards are not a form of money. The credit card company is merely promising to pay for the goods and services and the customer pays the credit card company later. These later payments involve the use of money.

ISBN: 9780170215718

1   The following items have all been used as money. Outline when and under what circumstances they could have been used.
    a   chocolate
    b   salt (from which the word 'salary' is derived)
    c   cowrie shells
    d   butter
    e   cigarettes

2   a   Construct a star diagram of the functions of money.
    b   Construct a star diagram of the characteristics of money.

3   Explain the difference in meaning between the functions of money and the characteristics of money.

The link between money and prices: The Quantity Theory of Money

The Quantity Theory of Money is an economic model used to show the link between the amount of money circulating in an economy and prices (i.e. inflation).
    A simple circular flow model illustrates this relationship.

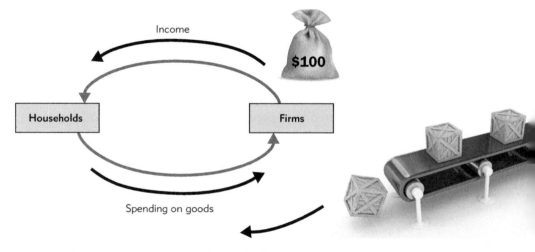

Imagine: 1   Our economy has only households and producers.
            2   Our economy produces four identical items a year (all crated up).

The firms pay the households for the factors of production. The households use this money to pay for the goods from the firms (the four crates). In this example the money has circulated ONCE in the year, from firms to households and then back to firms.

Let's also imagine that the money stock in this example is $100, then you can see that the workers were paid $100 and that the goods that they bought were worth $100.

The money stock (M) = the value of the goods.

The value of the goods is $100 but as there are four identical crates, we could calculate the price of each crate as $25.

The money stock (M) = price of each good (P) x number of goods (Q) (real output)

Let's imagine in another example that the money circulates more than once in a year. Let's imagine the money circulates four times in the year; *each time* firms pay households $100 for their labour and the households buy four crates from firms. (In total the households buy 16 crates, four crates four times.)

So now we have:

The money stock (M) x number of times the money circulates (V) =
price of each good (P) x number of goods (Q)
$$\$100 \times 4 = 25 \times 16$$

This relationship between the money stock and prices is known as the **Quantity Theory of Money**. It is expressed most simply as:

$$\textbf{MV = PQ}$$

This is known as the **Exchange Equation**.

If we assume that the number of times the money goes around (V) never changes, then our relationship is simplified to

M is proportional to PQ

which suggests that any change in M will result in a proportional change in PQ, i.e. if M rises, then PQ will also rise.

If we also assume that the number of goods produced or output (Q) never changes, then our relationship is simplified even further to

M is proportional to P

The money stock is proportional to the price level. This relationship is known as the **Crude Quantity Theory of Money**.

which suggests any change in M will result in a proportional change in P, i.e. if M rises, then P will also rise.

Increasing the money supply will increase prices. Even though we have more money, our purchasing power is no greater. We are no richer.

The *Crude Quantity Theory of Money* assumes that neither V nor Q can change and thus M is directly proportional to P. The relationship shows that increases in the money stock will cause inflation. If the money stock is doubled then the price level will also double.

This Crude Theory requires both V and Q to remain unchanged. Is it reasonable to assume Q, real output, cannot change?

ISBN: 9780170215718

The graph below shows New Zealand, Australia and USA real output levels over the past 20 years.

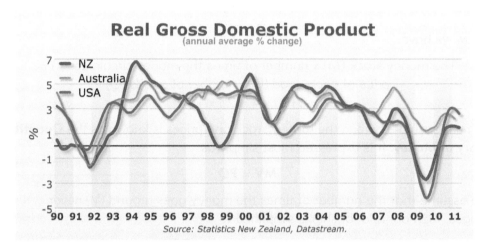

Real Gross Domestic Product
(annual average % change)

Source: Statistics New Zealand, Datastream.

It is clear that Q, real output, can change over time. This means that the assumption that Q is constant is a weakness. The **Sophisticated Quantity Theory of Money** was developed to help overcome this weakness. This version assumes that only V, the velocity of circulation, is constant; Q is able to change. The Sophisticated Quantity Theory of Money can be shown as:

M is proportional to PQ (V is still considered constant)

Here a change in the money stock (M) will result in a change in PQ. What is not clear is whether P will change, Q will change, or a combination of both will change.

With this in mind, if the money stock was to double then (P x Q) would also have to double, but the change could be made up of P doubling or Q doubling or some combination of the two. This suggests that the real output could soak up some of the inflationary pressure caused by the increase in money stock.

ACTIVITY

1 **a** Identify each component of the equation MV = PQ.
 b Explain what each component represents.
2 State the assumption(s) of the Crude Quantity Theory of Money.
3 Explain how an increase in the money stock will affect the price level according to the Crude Quantity Theory of Money.
4 State the assumption(s) of the Sophisticated Quantity Theory of Money.
5 Explain how an increase in the money stock will affect the price level according to the Sophisticated Theory of Money.
6 Explain what would happen if the government printed more money (i.e. increased the money stock) and gave a million dollars to every New Zealander.

ISBN: 9780170215718

Some knowledge of when the economy is likely to be able to change its output is useful.

- When an economy is operating near its full capacity, all resources and technology are being fully utilised, and output is unlikely to be able to increase to help offset the increase in money stock. The economy lacks the spare resources required to produce the extra output. So real output cannot increase when the money stock is increased. This means the price level will increase, however, when the money stock is increased.
- If the economy is not near full utilisation, then there are resources available to be used to produce more output. If the economy is not near full capacity then there are resources (labour and capital) available to be used to produce more output. It is possible for an increase in the money stock to be absorbed by increases in output, rather than result in an increase in the price level.

The business cycle

Economic activity follows a cyclical pattern over time. As an economy experiences an upturn/recovery, the level of economic activity increases, i.e. output rises and unemployment falls. This means resources become more fully utilised, so there are fewer and fewer opportunities to increase output further. Any increase in the money stock (M) will become more inflationary as output (Q) reaches full capacity.

After the economy peaks (boom), then economic activity will begin to decline (a downturn). Resources become more available as output falls and unemployment rises. A rise in money stock (M) may be absorbed by rises in output (Q) rather than resulting in increased prices.

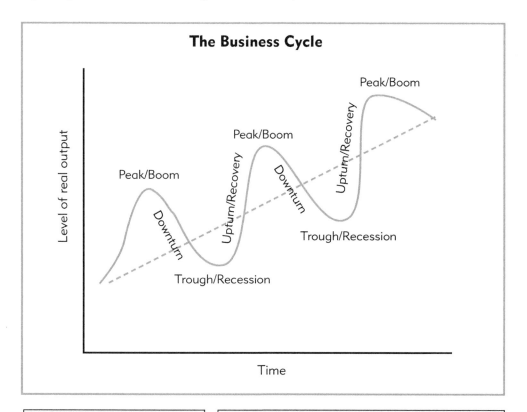

The Business Cycle

A **recession**: when Real GDP falls for two successive quarters.	A **depression**: while generally understood to be a severe recession it has no strict economic definition.

ISBN: 9780170215718

ACTIVITY

1 Fully explain why increases in money supply may or may not impact on prices.
   • Refer to the Quantity Theory of Money.
   • Refer to the business cycle.

2 Copy the diagram below and use it to illustrate the Quantity Theory of Money.

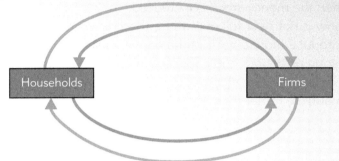

3

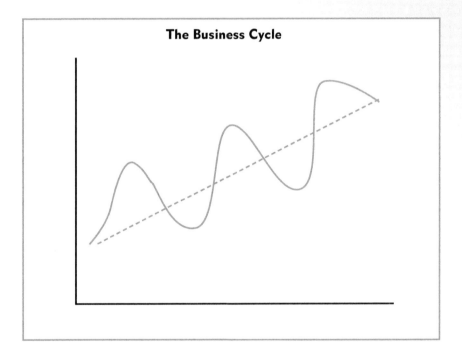

The Business Cycle

a Copy the diagram above. Fully label the graph and key points on the curve.

b Explain how where an economy is on the business cycle can affect the impact that changes in money supply have on the price level.

5 ■ An Economic Model of Inflation: AS/AD Model

By the end of this unit you will be able to:

- Explain the AS/AD model.
- Use the AS/AD model to illustrate cost-push and demand-pull inflation.
- Explain the nature of cost-push and demand-pull inflation.

Inflation is a rise in the general level of prices. The Quantity Theory of Money gives one reason, increases in the money supply, for a rise in the general level of prices. This is not the only reason. Other causes can generally be grouped as either **cost-push inflation** or **demand-pull inflation**. The **Aggregate Demand and Aggregate Supply (AD/AS) Model** can be used to illustrate both cost-push and demand-pull inflation.

Aggregate demand

Aggregate means total. Thus **aggregate demand** means the total demand and **aggregate supply** means total supply. The aggregate demand curve shows the total demand in an economy **at each price level**. The term **price level** is important as it is used to differentiate between a **price** (demand and supply model) and **general** or **overall** prices. Aggregate demand is the demand from each of the sectors of the economy as illustrated by the circular flow model.

> To illustrate a change in the general or overall level of prices, we need a model that incorporates general price levels. The simple supply and demand model deals with only one price in one particular market, NOT overall price level — it is an inadequate tool for this type of analysis.

> **AD = consumption/household spending (C) + investment spending (I) + government spending (G) + net exports (X - M)**
>
> **= C + I + G + (X - M)**

If any one of these components increases, then AD will increase and cause the AD curve to shift to the right.

If any one of these components decreases, then AD will decrease and the AD curve will shift to the left.

This is summarised below:

Inward shift (AD1 → AD3)
- Consumption/household spending falls
- Government spending falls
- Investment falls
- Net exports fall

Outward shift (AD1 → AD2)
- Consumption/household spending rises
- Government spending rises
- Investment rises
- Net exports rise

ISBN: 9780170215718

Aggregate supply

The aggregate supply curve shows the total output in an economy *at each price level*.

The aggregate supply curve is drawn **assuming that:**

- Nominal wages
- Import prices
  (cost of imported raw materials)
- Productivity

} are held constant.

If any of these factors change, then a new AS curve is drawn for each price level, e.g. if nominal wages rise, then at each output level a higher price is required to cover the increased costs of production. These factors are summarised below:

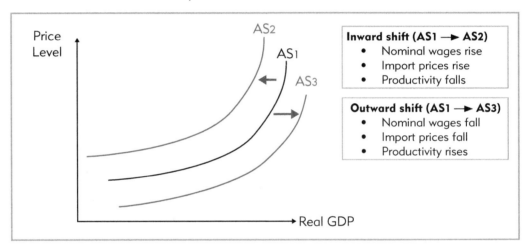

Aggregate demand and aggregate supply (AD/AS) model

Demand-pull inflation

Any factor causing a rise in AD, that is, a shift to the right of the AD curve, will cause a rise in the general level of prices. This is **DEMAND-PULL inflation.**

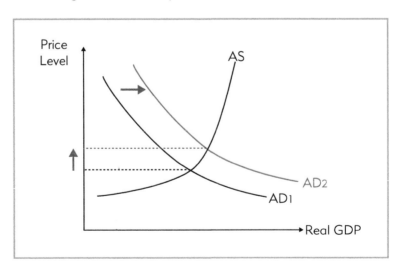

ISBN: 9780170215718

Why might consumption/household spending, government spending, investment spending or net exports change?

Households

Consumption/household spending (C) is affected by:

Disposable income: Increases in disposable income, through decreases in income tax, will increase household spending.

Interest rates: If interest rates fall, debt servicing (e.g. cost of mortgages) is cheaper. Credit spending will also increase, for example hire purchase.

Inflationary expectations: If consumers anticipate a rise in prices, they will buy now in order to avoid the higher price in the future. This will cause an increase in household spending in the present.

Government

Government spending (G) is affected by:

Elections: A change in government results in a change in policy regarding government spending. Generally, left-wing governments have traditionally been more likely to spend on social welfare and social infrastructure.

Firms

Investment spending (I) is affected by:

Interest rates: Lower interest rates lower the cost of borrowing or investing. It is more likely you will earn a profit on your investment if the financing cost of that investment is lower.

Business confidence: This is a measure of how firms perceive the economic outlook. High confidence means firms anticipate a positive future. Investment is likely to earn rewards in future profit, so is likely to increase.

Overseas

Net exports (X - M) are affected by:

Exchange rate: A fall in the New Zealand exchange rate will cause net exports to rise, as our exports are now relatively cheaper overseas. Conversely, imports are relatively more expensive if the New Zealand dollar depreciates. An increase in **interest rates** is likely to increase overseas investment in New Zealand. This will increase the demand for New Zealand dollars and thus the exchange rate will rise.

Overseas demand: Factors affecting our overseas markets may change, for instance our export markets may experience an economic boom period. This will increase demand from overseas and so increase net exports.

ISBN: 9780170215718

Economics for NCEA Level 2

1 Classify the following events as either **Increases AD**, **Decreases AD** or **Does not affect AD**.

a Emigration increases

b Price level increases

c Income tax is reduced

d Business confidence falls

e Recent immigration trends see New Zealand's population rise

f There is a reduction in savings by New Zealanders

g Investment levels rise

h The NZ$ appreciates

i New Zealand's major trading partners suffer a recession

2 For each of the events above explain how it affects AD.

3 Identify five possible causes for the demand-pull inflation shown in the graph below.

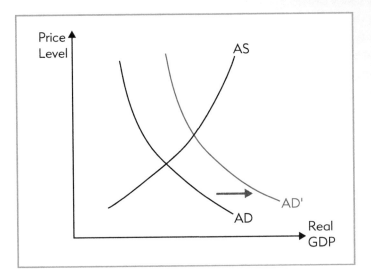

Cost-push inflation

Any factor causing a fall in AS, that is, a shift to the left of the AS curve, will cause a rise in the general level of prices. This is **COST-PUSH inflation**.

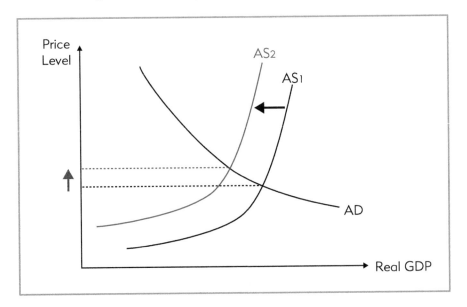

Explaining changes in aggregate supply

Why would nominal wages, import prices and productivity change?

Nominal wages

Nominal wages are likely to rise in response to worker efforts to increase and maintain standards of living. Increases in nominal wages cause cost-push inflation.

Cost of imported raw materials

Import prices change in response to exchange rate changes and inflationary pressure overseas. Increases in import costs cause cost-push inflation.

Productivity

Productivity rises through improved technology (better methods of production). Improved productivity *lowers* the price level.

> **Terminology Alert**
>
> **Nominal wages:** the actual dollar value of the wage. The face value of the wage.
>
> **Real wages:** the value of the wage adjusted for inflation. It is the purchasing power of the wage.

ACTIVITY

1 Classify the following events as either **Increases AS**, **Decreases AS** or **Does not affect AS**.
   a Productivity gains are achieved by New Zealand firms
   b Exchange rates fall
   c Nominal wages rise
   d Business confidence improves
   e Threat of war in the Middle East sees oil prices soar
   f New Zealand removes all remaining barriers to imports, e.g. tariffs
   g Investment levels rise
   h The NZ$ appreciates
   i New Zealand's cost of imports rises

2 For each of the events above explain how it affects AS.

3 Draw a fully labelled AD/AS diagram illustrating demand-pull inflation.

4 Draw a fully labelled AD/AS diagram illustrating cost-push inflation.

5 Identify three possible causes for the cost-push inflation shown in the graph below.

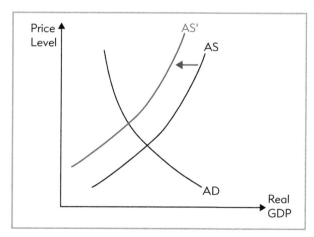

6 Fully explain the difference between demand-pull and cost-push inflation.

ISBN: 9780170215718

Economics for NCEA Level 2

Interpreting the AS/AD model

So far in our analysis we have been using the AS/AD model to look at inflation. The model also gives an opportunity to look at output (Real GDP) and employment. From here we can see the state of an economy by using our knowledge of the business cycle.

In the graph below a new line has been added to the model. This is the full employment output level. This is the output level that can be sustained when all resources are fully utilised, i.e. there is full employment. It is labelled Y_F.

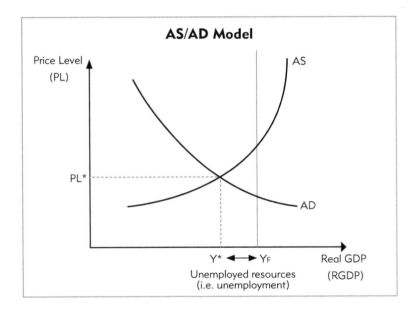

An economy is operating at the equilibrium point (PL*, Y*) on the model. This level of output is shown on the horizontal axis. By looking at the difference between this level of output and the full level of output we can judge whether the economy is experiencing high or low unemployment.

Once we know if there is high or low unemployment we can judge whether this is a boom (when all resources are fully utilised) or an economic trough (when there are many idle or unemployed resources). This can then be linked back to our Quantity Theory of Money model to judge the impact of changes in the money supply on the current rate of inflation.

ISBN: 9780170215718

Example: The two graphs below indicate two economies operating at below the full employment level. Graph A shows the economy is almost at full employment whereas in Graph B the economy is operating at well below the full employment level.

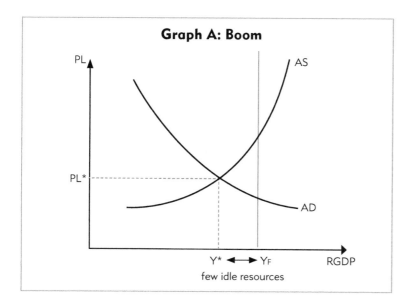

Graph A: Boom

Graph A: At near full employment
There are very few idle resources.
The economy is experiencing a BOOM.
According to the Quantity Theory of Money any increases in the money supply will not result in increases in the output level but will be inflationary.

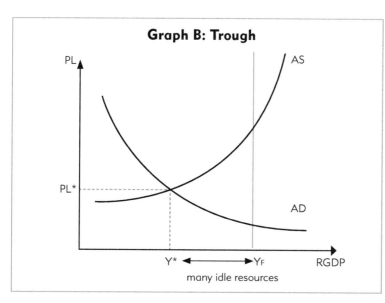

Graph B: Trough

Graph B: Well below full employment
There are many idle resources.
The economy is experiencing an economic TROUGH.
According to the Quantity Theory of Money any increases in the money supply could result in increases in the output level and so need not be inflationary.

ISBN: 9780170215718

ACTIVITY

a State the effect of demand-pull inflation on output levels.
b State the effect of cost-push inflation on output levels.
c Explain the link between output levels and employment levels.
d Fully explain which type of inflation is likely to concern a government.

6 ■ The Impacts of Inflation

By the end of this unit you will be able to:

- Analyse the impacts of changes in inflation on various groups in New Zealand society.

Inflation was a very important economic issue in the 1970s and 1980s but by the 1990s many of the developed economies had moved to control it. New Zealand experienced **price stability** (a low level of inflation) for many years, but recently inflation has reappeared as a significant pressure in the economy. This unit looks at inflation's effects on households and firms and income distribution.

What about interest earned on savings?

The rate quoted on your savings is the **nominal rate of interest**. For example, a bank may offer 8% p.a. interest on a term deposit — this figure is a nominal figure and you will receive 8% of the value of your savings each year you save. Remember, though, that what you can buy with the extra 8% is shrinking over time as prices rise.

The **real rate of interest** shows the purchasing power of the interest you earn. It is nominal interest rate adjusted for price changes.

Formula

$$\text{nominal rate of interest} - \text{inflation rate} = \text{real rate of interest}$$

This is the **real return** on your savings — this return can be negative, i.e. even after earning interest you are worse off.

Example

An interest rate of 7% p.a. at a time when annual inflation is running at 2.9% will mean your real rate of interest is

$$7 - 2.9 = 4.1\% \text{ p.a.}$$

Although you receive 7% p.a. from the bank, the value of the interest has been eroded by prices rising while you saved.

The purchasing power of money

The ability to buy goods and services is your **purchasing power**.

Inflation erodes the value of money. As prices rise the money you hold can buy fewer and fewer goods and services. The ability to buy goods and services is reduced by inflation. We call this a reduction in your purchasing power.

Households

The key impacts of inflation are on households' borrowing and saving.

Disincentive to save

Inflation erodes the **purchasing power of money**. When prices rise, the same amount of money buys less and less. There is no point in saving money if your $100 bank deposit may have bought you a pair of jeans in 2000 but in 2005 price rises mean you can no longer afford them. It would have been better to purchase them back in 2000. In periods of inflation there is no reason to save your money.

Erosion of the value of existing savings

Any savings you have are losing purchasing power.

Incentive to borrow

The amount borrowed, while remaining nominally the same, has fallen in real terms. Many people borrow heavily in times of high inflation to buy property in the hope of making a capital gain and using inflation to decrease the real value of the debt.

ISBN: 9780170215718

1 Identify the groups most likely to be hurt by a loss in value of their savings (i.e. the households that save in an economy) and the groups most likely to be helped by a loss of the value of their debt (i.e. the households that borrow in an economy).

2 Copy and complete this table.

Year	2008	2009	2010	2011	2012	2013
Nominal interest rate	3.0	3.5	2.5		6.75	5.25
Inflation rate	2.4	2.7		3.5	6.0	8.7
Real interest rate			0.6	3.0		

- Low rates of savings and high rates of borrowing for residential property purchases have been identified as one of the key problems for New Zealand growth, **as it reduces available investment in the productive sector**.
- **Fiscal drag** is a phenomenon associated with inflation when the income tax regime is **progressive**. A progressive tax regime is one where the percentage paid on a dollar earned increases as incomes rise. For example:

> Inflation ↑
> Savings ↓
> Investment ↓
> Growth ↓

On the first $20 000 you may pay 20% tax (20 cents in every dollar earned).
On the second $20 000 you may pay 30% tax (30 cents in every dollar you earned over $20 000).
On all other income above $40 000 you may pay 40% tax (40 cents in every dollar earned above $40 000).

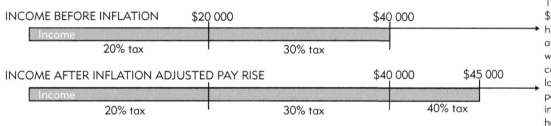

INCOME BEFORE INFLATION $20 000 $40 000
Income
        20% tax   30% tax

INCOME AFTER INFLATION ADJUSTED PAY RISE $40 000 $45 000
Income
        20% tax   30% tax   40% tax

The increase of $5000 is taxed at the higher rate so although your income was adjusted to compensate for the loss of purchasing power due to inflation, the tax rise has partly undermined this adjustment.

If wage rates are rising to compensate for rises in prices, your wage increase may move you up into higher and higher tax brackets. If your wage rate is just matching inflation, you are paying a higher proportion in tax, effectively making you worse off. This is **fiscal drag**. New Zealand operates a progressive tax regime for income tax.

> Inflation ↑
> Fiscal drag ↑
> Motivation to work ↓
> Productivity ↓
> Growth ↓

Firms

The key impacts of inflation are on **costs**, **planning** and **investment**. The volatile nature of high inflation means costs and revenues are unpredictable. Firms take a conservative approach to investment and thus levels fall.

ISBN: 9780170215718

Inflation ↑
Investment ↓
Growth ↓

Inflation ↑
Exports ↓ and Imports ↑
Trade balance ↓
(i.e. Trade deficit
increases)

- The key to growth is investment levels and these are negatively affected by high inflation. This will affect the availability of jobs and wage rates.
- In periods of high inflation, trade is harmed:
  Exports — the prices of our products rise so we are increasingly less competitive compared with our trading partners — expect exports to fall.
  Imports — less expensive imported goods are increasingly attractive compared to our goods — expect imports to rise.
  Overall, expect our Balance on Goods to fall = larger deficit.

Income distribution

Inflation causes a transfer of wealth from savers to borrowers. People on fixed incomes (e.g. beneficiaries) suffer more than those whose incomes adjust with inflation. Expect the gap between rich and poor to widen.

ACTIVITY

1 Identify the groups most likely to be on a fixed income and the groups most likely to be able to increase wages in line with, or faster than, inflation.

2 Compare and contrast the effect of increasing rates of inflation on:
  a savers
  b borrowers.

3 Many people rely on interest on their savings for their income. They are hurt by low interest rates. Explain how this statement can be both true and false. (CLUE: Use the terms nominal and real interest rates in your answer.)

'So make no mistake: controlling inflation is about helping people, and making it easier for people to plan their lives. And to the surprise of many people, it turns out that it is not so much the rich that are most advantaged by controlling inflation as the poor, since, like most taxes, inflation is a tax that the poor find particularly hard to avoid.'

'Making Monetary Policy: A Look Behind the Curtains', speech by Dr Donald T. Brash, Governor RBNZ, 26 January 2001

4 Explain the acronym RBNZ.

5 Explain the term 'Governor RBNZ'.

6 Identify the period Dr Donald Brash was the governor of the RBNZ.

7 Identify the current governor of the RBNZ.

8 Explain why the poor are likely to be more disadvantaged than the rich by inflation, as Dr Brash suggests.

ISBN: 9780170215718

7 ■ Government Policy and Inflation

By the end of this unit you will be able to:

- Give examples of policies that would modify the impact of inflation.
- Give examples of policies that would modify the causes of inflation.
- Evaluate policies which aim to modify the impact of inflation.
- Evaluate policies which aim to modify the causes of inflation.

The government has made achieving price stability the primary target of its monetary policy. It also ensured the Reserve Bank of New Zealand could achieve this independently of the government when it enacted the Reserve Bank Act 1989. While this is its current strategy, it is by no means the only option open to government.

There are two basic approaches to dealing with inflation:

1 Tackling the impacts of inflation.
2 Tackling the causes of inflation.

Tackling the impact of inflation will do nothing to get rid of inflation itself. It merely treats its effects. The second approach will, if successful, contain or remove the inflation. However the effects of the inflation will remain until the rising price levels are brought under control.

Targeting the impact of inflation

1 **Indexation:** Incomes, particularly those fixed by government (for example, superannuation), and other benefits are linked to the CPI and adjusted to ensure purchasing power is maintained.

Evaluation: One of the limitations of the CPI is that it measures an average price rise, thus the price rises experienced by the indexed household or individual may not match CPI. Also, increasing these incomes may fuel inflation as these groups increase their demand for goods and services.

> **Monetary Policy**
> Using the money supply to achieve government objectives.

2 **Price freezes** (possibly coupled with a wage freeze): Here, prices are frozen by regulation. The price freeze is a price maximum which leads to shortages and, possibly, black markets. *Evaluation:* Problems of price maximums are experienced. When the freeze is lifted, prices rise suddenly to the market equilibrium.

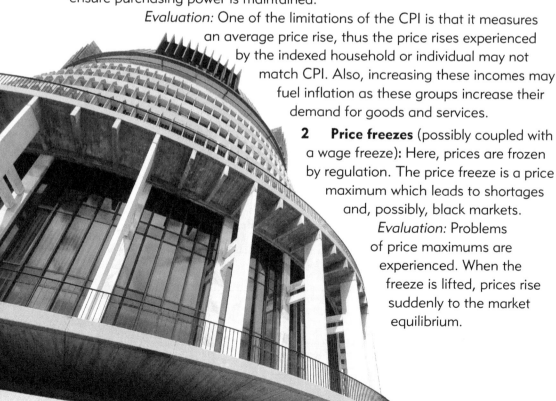

ISBN: 9780170215718

ACTIVITY

1 Outline the impacts of inflation

2 Outline the causes of inflation. You may like to review units 4 and 6 to remind you.

3 Explain the difference between 'tackling the impacts of inflation' and 'tackling the causes of inflation'.

4 Explain why a price freeze may control inflation in the short term, but when the controls are lifted the effect is likely to be high inflation.

Targeting the causes of inflation

Rather than imposing a price freeze, governments now control rising prices through less direct methods. In New Zealand this is done by manipulating interest rates. This flow chart outlines how this works.

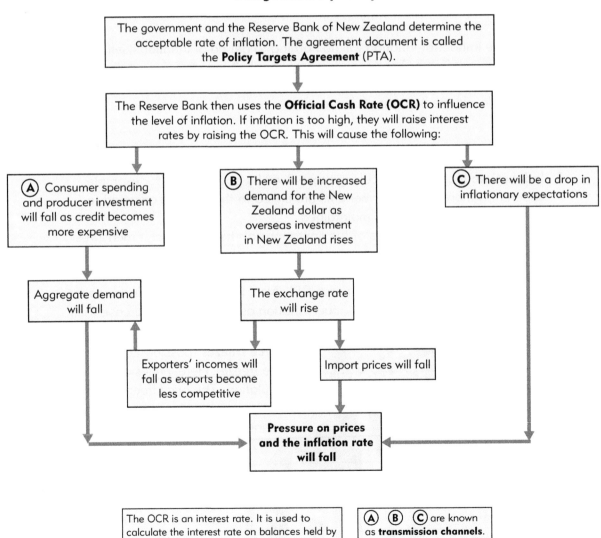

Government Influence on the Rate of Inflation in New Zealand Using Monetary Policy

The government and the Reserve Bank of New Zealand determine the acceptable rate of inflation. The agreement document is called the **Policy Targets Agreement** (PTA).

The Reserve Bank then uses the **Official Cash Rate (OCR)** to influence the level of inflation. If inflation is too high, they will raise interest rates by raising the OCR. This will cause the following:

(A) Consumer spending and producer investment will fall as credit becomes more expensive

(B) There will be increased demand for the New Zealand dollar as overseas investment in New Zealand rises

(C) There will be a drop in inflationary expectations

Aggregate demand will fall

The exchange rate will rise

Exporters' incomes will fall as exports become less competitive

Import prices will fall

Pressure on prices and the inflation rate will fall

The OCR is an interest rate. It is used to calculate the interest rate on balances held by banks with the Reserve Bank. This in turn determines the interest rates consumers receive on balances, or pay on mortgages and credit cards.

(A) (B) (C) are known as **transmission channels**.

The use of monetary policy to control inflation was introduced in 1984 but using the OCR was introduced in 1999. The OCR is the 'overnight cost' of money for banks. All banks are required to hold deposits at the Reserve Bank called **settlement cash**. These deposits are used to 'settle' the transactions between the banks. These are the only balances that can be used for this purpose.

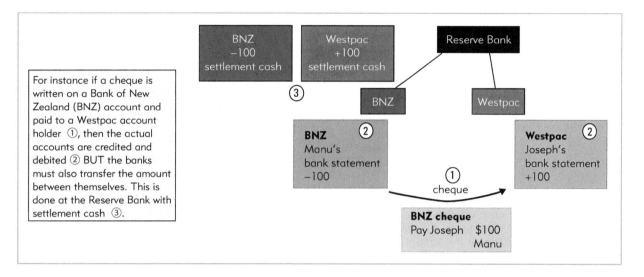

For instance if a cheque is written on a Bank of New Zealand (BNZ) account and paid to a Westpac account holder ①, then the actual accounts are credited and debited ② BUT the banks must also transfer the amount between themselves. This is done at the Reserve Bank with settlement cash ③.

If a bank has a positive balance at the Reserve Bank, at the end of the day they will earn the OCR less 0.25% interest on this balance. If a bank does not have enough settlement cash to meet its requirements, it must borrow from the Reserve Bank, paying the OCR plus 0.25%. The other banks with positive settlement cash balances could also lend for these settlement balances. However they will not lend it for less than the OCR less 0.25% they are earning on this balance, and the bank looking for a loan will not pay more than the OCR plus 0.25% they receive from the Reserve Bank. This means the cost of overnight money is effectively pinned at the OCR plus or minus 0.25%. Thus the Reserve Bank is controlling the price of money. Banks must lend to their customers at rates higher than this rate in order to make a positive return.

The Reserve Bank assesses inflationary pressures and sets the OCR to control the price changes expected in the following 18 months, with the aim of achieving the inflation levels determined by government. These are usually in the range of 1–3%.

ACTIVITY

1 Web check (www.rbnz.govt.nz). Inflation targets were set when the Reserve Bank Act and its Policy Targets Agreements were established in 1989. There have been three targets set to date. Identify the targets since 1989.
2 Explain what PTA stands for.
3 Identify the signatories to the PTA.
4 a Explain what is meant by 'monetary policy'.
  b Identify who implements monetary policy in New Zealand.
  c Identify the prime objective of monetary policy in New Zealand.
5 Explain how an increase in interest rates affects prices.
6 Explain how high and volatile inflation affects firms.
7 Compare and contrast the effect of controlling inflation through interest rate rises on:
  a Firms   b Households.

ISBN: 9780170215718

Inflation buys only short-term benefits

By SIMON CARLAW*

The period during and just after the election has seen some debate over inflation, including what sort of arrangement the Finance Minister should establish with the new Reserve Bank Governor.

This debate has included charges that the Reserve Bank has been too rigid, fixated on the target range's mid-point, and that a 'smoothing' of monetary policy changes is required, with the implication that the upper range of the target could be stretched just a little bit to help get some more growth in the economy.

This implication can seem attractive at face value, but there are dangers in allowing 'just a bit more inflation' to become entrenched. Yes, a bit more inflation might help us grow in nominal terms in the short term (but not necessarily in real terms); it could boost job growth (but only in the short term); it could even give exporters a lower exchange rate (but even this is debatable).

But before too long the resulting price increases would cause a reduction in real wages, since those wages would buy less. The pressure for compensatory increases in wages and salaries would lead to further price increases, and the inflationary spiral would be all on again. No one wants to go back to the tough medicine of the mid-80s that was required to bring double-digit inflation to heel.

The recent debate also seems to have flushed out an important point, that the Reserve Bank has, in fact, not been fixated on the target's mid-point (1.5 per cent), the evidence pointing to an average rate just below 3 per cent. If anything, it could be argued that the Reserve Bank has been overly generous.

But what about the charge that our monetary policy needs smoothing? This suggestion would entail smaller, more gradual changes in the official cash rate (OCR) over a longer period. The issue was addressed by Professor Lars Svensson's recent Review of the Operation of Monetary Policy, in which he suggested the Reserve Bank's policy targets agreement should be amended to provide for an explicit medium-term target.

This is a useful suggestion. Changes to monetary conditions, that is, easing or tightening, can often take 18 months to two years to have their full effect on the economy. But the wording of the agreement, which mandates a target of 12-monthly increases in the CPI of 0–3 per cent, could imply a short-term focus and encourage overly rapid and/or pronounced easing or tightening of monetary conditions.

Having an explicit medium-term rather than an implicit 12-month target period might lessen the need for aggressive monetary management such as during 1999–2000, when the OCR rocketed from 4.5 per cent to 6.5 per cent within six months. Such volatility in interest rates can cause currency volatility.

Currency volatility impacts sharply on small exporters. Most of our exporters are small.

Small businesses often find it difficult or impractical to hedge and so find themselves exposed to occasionally large and sudden fluctuations in the currency.

These fluctuations are no worse than for many other currencies — IMF statistics indicate that between 1989 and last year the New Zealand dollar was no more volatile than Australian, Canadian, UK and US currencies. But that's still pretty volatile: the effective exchange rate on the US dollar rose more than 30 per cent between 1995 and this year; the Australian dollar depreciated by a similar amount between 1997 and this year.

What happens to small firms in times of currency volatility? They are in danger of going under.

A survey by the Manufacturers' Federation in 1999 showed an 11 per cent decline in the numbers of small exporting firms in the previous two years — a period when interest and exchange rates rose and fell dramatically — accompanied by anecdotal evidence that periods of sudden appreciation in the New Zealand dollar have caused many smaller firms to cease exporting.

One story is instructive. A Wellington manufacturer, exporting to Australia in the mid-90s, got caught in the crossfire as the NZ dollar appreciated by 32 per cent. His product became too expensive and his clients switched to other suppliers.

'We just had to walk away from the Australian market,' he says. 'You can't get the client back when the dollar drops again — they want price stability, too.'

Since then he's become an importer and a manufacturer for the domestic market only — it's safer that way.

Price stability isn't the only prerequisite for growth; it's one of several policy levers, enabling the other levers to work more efficiently and encouraging the private sector to invest, spend and save with confidence.

Without price stability, investment becomes uncertain, and without investment there can be no growth. That's why it's worth debating the technical aspects of monetary policy — because of the impact on growth. But the technical debate should not overshadow this more fundamental issue.

*At the time this article was written, Simon Carlaw was chief executive of Business New Zealand.

ISBN: 9780170215718

Read the article on page 48 to answer the questions below.

8 Explain the term inflationary spiral.

9 Copy the AS/AD model below. Use your graph to illustrate the effect of an inflationary spiral on price level and real output.

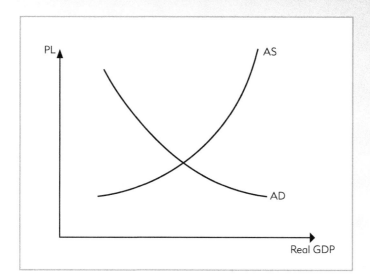

10 Higher interest rates will lower the price level.
   a Fully explain the three transmission channels that interest rates work through to affect the price level.
   b Illustrate these effects using the AS/AD model.

11 Explain why periods of high inflation will cause the RBNZ to raise interest rates.

12 Explain how changes in interest rates affect exchange rates.

13 Explain how an increase in the exchange rate hurts exporters.

14 Explain how price stability affects investment and growth.

15 Comment on the importance of price stability for New Zealand's economic outlook.

16 Are price stability and controlling inflation the same thing? Explain your answer.

ISBN: 9780170215718

Employment

1 ▪ Employment: Defining the Issue

By the end of this unit you will be able to:

- Identify statistical sources of employment and unemployment data.
- Define working age population and labour force.
- Relate employment and unemployment to population, working age population and labour force.
- Use the Production Possibility Frontier economic model to illustrate employment and unemployment of resources.

This unit explores some of the terms, concepts, models, causes and effects of employment. Rather than focusing on employment we look at unemployment and attempts to fix problems associated with it.

We begin with the problems of defining both employment and unemployment. It is an issue faced by economists, statisticians and governments the world over.

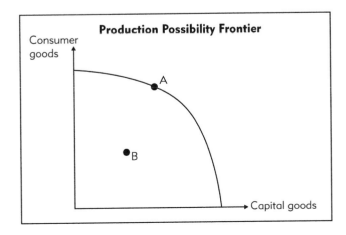

Employment and the Production Possibility Frontier

The **Production Possibility Frontier (PPF)** is an economic model which looks at the utilisation of resources and technology. It can be used to illustrate various employment concepts. The PPF shows the maximum output combinations with given **resources** and technology. **Workers are a resource** (human resources or labour).

Any point on the curve represents full

ISBN: 9780170215718

utilisation of resources and technology. In terms of labour this means full utilisation of workers or **full employment** (point A).

Any point inside the curve represents underutilisation of resources and technology. In terms of labour this means **unemployment** (point B).

This seems rather straightforward, but what is meant by *full employment* or *full utilisation of resources*? Does it mean everyone working 24, 12, 8 hours a day or 5, 6, 7 days a week? And what about highly trained individuals working below their potential as semi- or unskilled labour, or disabled individuals or a 20-year-old studying at a tertiary institution?

Generally 'employed' is taken to mean in **paid employment.** While this definition may appear reasonable, consider a person raising his or her own children. The person would be unemployed though a childcare worker performing the same function would be 'employed'.

A house husband is not employed

Another issue is that of **underemployment**. This is where someone is employed at a level below their full skill or training level, for instance doctors driving taxis or engineers waiting on tables. It is a problem faced by some new immigrants to New Zealand. Alternatively, underemployed can refer to those people working part-time but who would like to work more hours.

Underemployment

So while the PPF model illustrates broad ideas of employment and unemployment and the effect on output levels, it does not answer the questions of how to practically define either the full or underutilisation of resources with respect to labour.

Making a start: Population, the working age population and the labour force

The following definitions are used by Statistics New Zealand.

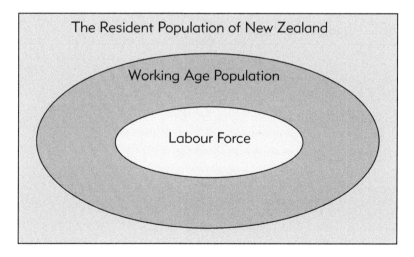

Working age population
The usually resident, non-institutionalised civilian population of New Zealand aged 15 years and over.

ISBN: 9780170215718

Economics for NCEA Level 2

The labour force

People aged 15 years and over who regularly work for one or more hours per week for financial gain, are unpaid working in a family business, or who are unemployed and seeking either full- or part-time work. The **full-time labour force** comprises persons working 30 hours or more per week and unemployed persons seeking full-time work. The **part-time labour force** comprises persons working one to 29 hours per week and unemployed persons seeking part-time work.

It is the **labour force** that is considered either employed or unemployed. The unemployment rate is the proportion of the labour force that is unemployed:

$$\left(\frac{\text{unemployed}}{\text{labour force}} \times \frac{100}{1} \right)$$

ACTIVITY

1 The labour force is a subset of the working age population. Explain who might be in the working age population but not in the labour force.

2 **a** Using the data provided below calculate the unemployment rates in New Zealand for the period 2000–2010.

 b Graph your results.

 c Comment on the trends shown on your graph.

Year	Resident population (000)	Working age population (000)	Employed (000)	Unemployed (000)	Labour force (000)
2000	3873	2994	1784	124	1908
2001	3916	3036	1824	106	1930
2002	3989	3103	1894	106	2000
2003	4062	3171	1930	101	2031
2004	4114	3223	1994	89	2083
2005	4161	3273	2066	83	2149
2006	4211	3324	2124	89	2213
2007	4252	3364	2167	86	2253
2008	4292	3402	2199	105	2304
2009	4347	3454	2158	158	2316
2010	4394	3498	2157	157	2314

ISBN: 9780170215718

2 ▪ Counting and Measuring

By the end of this unit you will be able to:

- Identify the main statistical surveys used to measure employment and unemployment.
- Recognise that different definitions of unemployment and employment give rise to different measures of unemployment and employment.

The employed

The *Statistics New Zealand* surveys that measure employment are:

Up-to-date statistics can be found on the Statistics New Zealand website: www.stats.govt.nz

1 Quarterly Employment Survey
2 Household Labour Force Survey
3 The Census of Population and Dwellings

THE SURVEYS

The Quarterly Employment Survey (QES)

The QES is conducted every three months (quarterly) and surveys approximately 18 000 businesses from a range of industries and regions throughout New Zealand. The survey is designed to measure quarterly estimates of average hourly and average weekly (pre-tax) wages, average weekly paid hours and the number of filled jobs.

Source: Labour Market Statistics, *Statistics New Zealand*

The Household Labour Force Survey (HLFS)

The HLFS is based on a sample of about 15 000 private dwellings each quarter. This yields about 30 000 respondents every three months.
This survey began in 1985, so it has a **limited history of data**. However, it does meet the **internationally accepted standard** for measuring unemployment and is the **official measure**.

Source: Labour Market Statistics, *Statistics New Zealand*

ISBN: 9780170215718

Economics for NCEA Level 2

The Census of Population and Dwellings

A five yearly survey of all individuals resident in New Zealand on census night.

The largest possible sample size creates the best measure. However, the size of the data collection means that results take a **long time to compile. The definitions used in measuring unemployment have also changed.** In 1991 the definition of unemployed included a requirement of **actively seeking work** instead of merely **wanting work**. The employment definitions used in the census now match the HLFS definition, but **changes in definitions affect its usefulness in comparisons over time**.

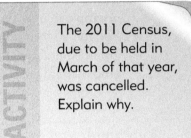

ACTIVITY

The 2011 Census, due to be held in March of that year, was cancelled. Explain why.

THE DEFINITIONS

The Quarterly Employment Survey (QES)

The Employed

Full-time/part-time
Full-time are those who regularly work 30 hours or more per week. Part-time are those who regularly work less than 30 hours per week.

Full-time equivalent employees (FTE)
The number of full-time employees plus half the number of part-time employees.

Filled jobs
Filled jobs comprise all full-time employees plus all part-time employees plus working proprietors in businesses that have employees. Filled jobs results measure the number of filled jobs, not the number of employed people. Individuals with more than one job are counted at each workplace.

The Census of Population and Dwellings AND Household Labour Force Survey

The Employed
A person is employed if he or she is in the working-age population and:

- Works for one hour or more for pay or profit in the context of an employee/employer relationship or self-employment.
- Works without pay for one hour or more in work that contributes directly to the operation of a farm, business or professional practice owned or operated by a relative.
- Had a job but is not at work due to:
  - illness or injury (his or her own)
  - personal or family responsibilities
  - bad weather or mechanical breakdown
  - direct involvement in industrial dispute
  - being on leave or on holiday.

Full-time: People who usually work 30 or more hours per week.
Part-time: People who usually work fewer than 30 hours per week.

ISBN: 9780170215718

Measuring the unemployed

The *Statistics New Zealand* surveys that measure unemployment are:

1 Household Labour Force Survey (this gives us the official measure of unemployment)
2 The Census of Population and Dwellings.

The Department of Labour, through Work and Income New Zealand (WINZ), produces the registered job-seekers statistics. However the job-seekers register is no longer used for reporting on unemployment because policy changes over the last ten years mean that numbers are not comparable over time.

The number of people receiving the unemployment benefit is also available from WINZ.

The Household Labour Force Survey AND Census of Population and Dwellings

The Unemployed
All people in the working-age population who are without a paid job, are available for work, and had actively sought work in the past four weeks ending with the reference week, or have a new job to start within four weeks.
A person whose only job-search method in the previous four weeks has been to look at job advertisements in the newspapers is not considered to be actively seeking work.

The Jobless
The jobless are defined as the officially unemployed, plus those people who are without employment and are either available but not actively seeking work, or actively seeking but not available for work.

It is important to realise that different definitions give rise to different figures.

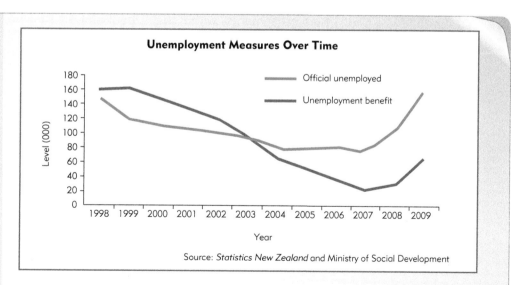

1 Outline the trends shown in the graph above.
2 Explain why these two measures of unemployment are not the same.
3 Explain how the jobless and the unemployed differ.

ISBN: 9780170215718

Economics for NCEA Level 2

The table below outlines the differences between the official unemployment figures (HLFS) and the unemployment benefit recipients.

Characteristic	Officially unemployed (from Household Labour Force Survey)	Unemployment benefit recipients
Age	15 years or over	18–64 years (generally)
Residency	'Usually resident'	Continuously lived in New Zealand for two years since becoming a citizen or permanent resident
Full-time or part-time work sought	Seeking work for one hour or more per week	Seeking full-time employment
Current work status	Less than one hour per week for pay or profit in the previous week, and have had no unpaid work in a relative's business	May work part-time subject to relevant income tests
Income	Not relevant	Ineligible if income is greater than a threshold
Partner's employment status	Not relevant	Makes some ineligible (through excess income)
In tertiary study	Can count as unemployed	Generally ineligible for unemployment benefit
Efforts to find work	Must have actively sought work (done more than checking newspaper advertisements) within the last four weeks	Complies with Jobseeker Agreement, work test and any other administrative requirements of Work and Income
Availability for work	Must be available for work within the next four weeks	May be unavailable for work for short periods
Wanting income assistance from Work and Income	Not relevant	Must apply for an unemployment benefit, and meet eligibility criteria
Timing	Quarterly average	Administrative count at month end

Source: Adapted from information from the Ministry for Social Development website www.msd.govt.nz

ISBN: 9780170215718

3 ■ Demand for Labour: An Economic Model

By the end of this unit you will be able to:

- Recognise the labour market as an example of a factor market.
- Outline the determinants of the demand for labour.

There are a range of markets within an economy. The market for goods and services is most apparent. Another is the market for factors of production or resources. The labour market is an example of one of these markets. The labour market is a factor market. As it is a market, the supply and demand model can be used to illustrate and analyse it.

The demand for labour

The demand for labour is a **derived demand**. It comes from the demand for the good or services produced. Derived means 'to come from'. The demand for a good or service is a **final demand**.

The demand for ice cream makers comes from or is derived from the demand for the good they produce, i.e. the demand for ice creams.

creates the demand for

The producers are the buyers of labour – they demand labour because of its role in the production process. The demand for labour shows the quantity of hours/workers/available jobs at any given wage rate, *ceteris paribus*.

ISBN: 9780170215718

The graph of the demand for labour

The graph shows the quantity of labour demanded (measured in hours) at each wage rate.

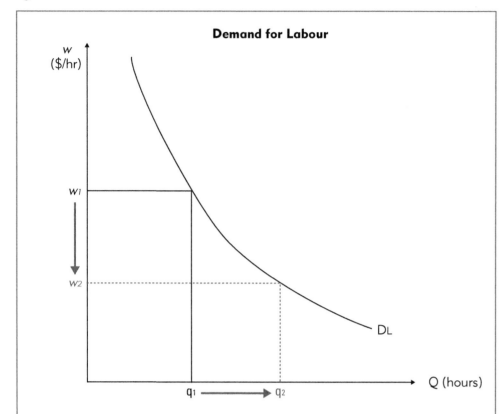

w = the wage rate. Wages are the price of labour or dollars paid per hour.
Q = the quantity of labour demanded by producers.

Any change in the wage rate causes a movement along the demand for labour curve.
A *decrease in wages* will result in a larger quantity of labour being demanded, *ceteris paribus* (shown).
An *increase in wages* will result in a smaller quantity of labour being demanded, *ceteris paribus*.

Relaxing *ceteris paribus*

Ceteris paribus means 'all other factors remain unchanged'.
The other factors that affect the demand for labour are:

- Changes in the final demand for the good or service the labour produces.
- Changes in technology or the productivity of labour.

A change in these factors will result in a shift of the demand for labour curve to the right (increase in the demand for labour) or left (decrease in the demand for labour) as shown in the graphs on the next page.

ISBN: 9780170215718

1 Changes in the final demand for the good or service the labour produces

Example: Decrease in the demand for hamburgers

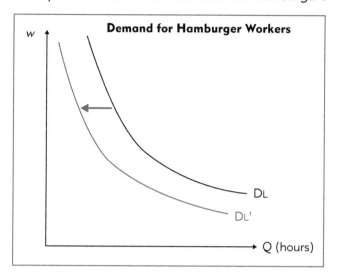

As fewer hamburgers are sold, fewer workers are required at each wage rate. The demand for labour will decrease. The graph will shift left.

2 Changes in technology or the productivity of labour

Example: Increase in labour productivity

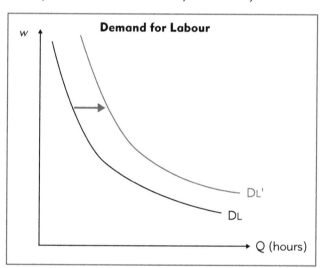

When more efficient technology is introduced, worker productivity increases so an employer will demand more workers at each wage rate. The demand for labour will increase. The graph will shift right.

ACTIVITY

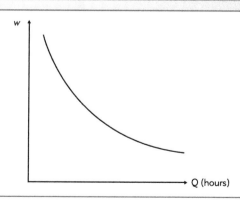

1 Copy the graph above and use it to show the effect of an increase in the final demand for scooters.

2 Copy the graph above and use it show the effect of a drop in labour productivity.

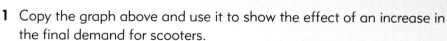

ISBN: 9780170215718

Changes in the final demand for goods and services

There are a range of reasons the final demand for a good or service may change.
They are listed below:

- A change in consumers' disposable income.
- Changes in the prices of related goods:
    - The price of complementary goods change.
    - The price of substitute goods change.
- Consumer tastes and preferences for goods and services change.
- Changes in population.

A change in disposable incomes

If disposable incomes are rising (perhaps because income taxes have fallen) then
people will buy more goods and services. This will mean there is an increased
demand for workers to make the extra goods.

    If disposable income rises the demand for iPads also rises.

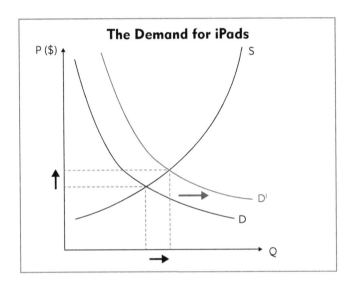

    This will cause a rise in the demand for workers in
iPad manufacturing.

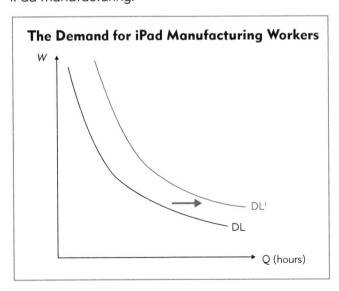

ISBN: 9780170215718

A change in the price of other goods

Substitute goods

Substitute goods are goods that can be used instead of another good, e.g. butter and margarine, or pizza and hamburgers. Consumers will switch to the relatively cheaper goods. The producers of the substitute will need more workers to meet the increase in demand. Conversely the original producer will require fewer workers.

This is particularly important when the substitute good is an imported good. The New Zealand producer requires fewer workers and the producer overseas requires more workers. New Zealand jobs are lost to overseas workers.

For example, the price of margarine falls, the demand for butter will fall and so the demand for dairy workers falls.

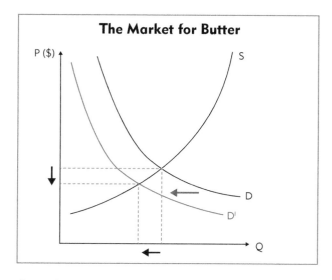

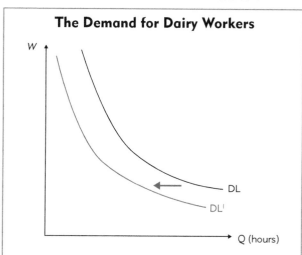

Complement goods

Complement goods are goods that can be used together with another good, e.g. MP3 player and online music. If the price of a complement good falls then consumers will buy more of that good (requiring more workers to make the goods) but it will also trigger a rise in the demand for complementary goods. This producer will demand more labour to produce extra goods as well.

For example, the price of online music falls, and so the demand for MP3 players will rise, the demand for MP3 manufacturing workers will rise.

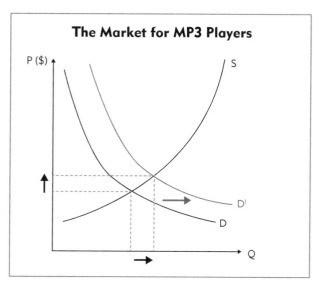

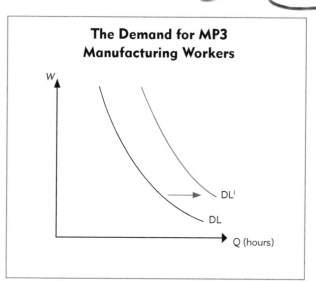

ISBN: 9780170215718

Economics for NCEA Level 2

Change in tastes and preferences

These represent a wide variety of reasons for consumer changes in demand. New innovative products on the market change our buying decisions, as do changes in tastes or fashions. For example, the trend toward 'green' or organic products has seen a greater range of these products become available and thus a greater number of workers involved in producing them.

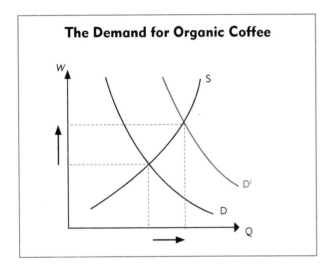

The Demand for Organic Coffee

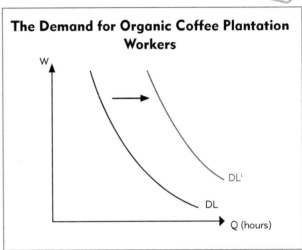

The Demand for Organic Coffee Plantation Workers

ACTIVITY

Copy and complete the table below.

Scenario	Change in the demand for labour: Increase or decrease?	Shift in the demand for labour curve left or right?	Explanation
a Increase in exports of wine			
b Increase in government spending			
c Rise in income tax rates			
d Increase in foreign investment in New Zealand sees new factories established			

ISBN: 9780170215718

ACTIVITY

e	Productivity rises through increased use of computer technology			
f	Emigration rises			
g	War on terrorism results in increased spending on security measures in New Zealand			
h	Free trade sees New Zealand flooded with imports			
i	Birth rate continues to fall			
j	World wide economic boom			

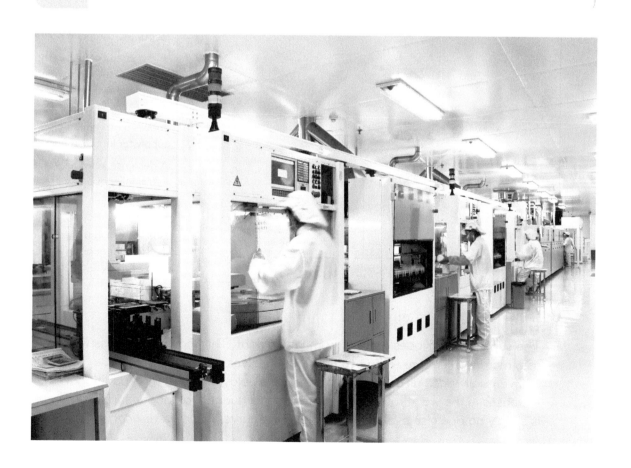

ISBN: 9780170215718

4 ▪ The Supply of Labour

By the end of this unit you will be able to:
- Explain the shape of the supply of labour curve.
- Outline the determinants of the supply of labour curve.
- Use the supply and demand model to illustrate the labour market.

The supply side of a market focuses on the seller. However there are some significant differences between the supply of a final commodity and the supply of a factor of production. Labour is supplied by the householders or consumers in return for wages. This makes the labour market, where demand and supply factors come together, particularly interesting.

The supply of labour
Households provide the supply of labour. The supply of labour shows the number of workers who are willing to work at each given wage rate.

The graph of the supply of labour
The graph below shows the quantity of labour supplied (measured in hours) at each wage rate.

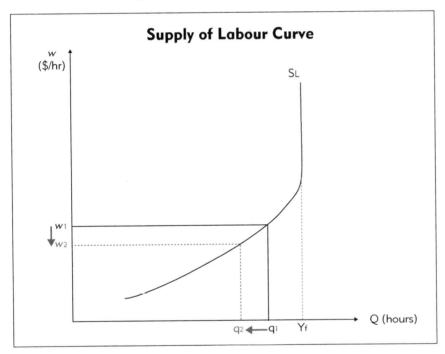

S_L = the number of workers willing to work at each wage rate.

w = the wage rate.

Q = the quantity supplied of labour (measured in hours).

Y_f = quantity of labour that represents full employment for this economy.

Any change in the wage rate causes a movement along the supply for labour curve.

A *decrease in wages* will result in a smaller quantity of labour being supplied, *ceteris paribus* (shown).

An *increase in wages* will result in a greater quantity of labour being supplied, *ceteris paribus*.

The shape of the supply of labour curve
The supply curve slopes upward from left to right. This indicates that as wages rise, more workers **are willing to make themselves available for work.**

Eventually once all available workers are employed (at Y_f) then additional increases in the wage rate cannot increase the quantity of labour supplied. There is simply no one else available to work so the curve becomes *vertical*.

ISBN: 9780170215718

It is also arguable that at very high wage rates workers may make themselves less available for work because they will start to substitute leisure for work. They can afford to do this on their high wage rates.

Relaxing ceteris paribus

Ceteris paribus means 'all other factors remain unchanged'.

The other factors that affect the supply for labour are:

- Changes in the size of the population:
  - Net migration/Rate of natural increase.
- Changes in the size of the labour force:
  - School leaving age/Compulsory retirement age/Attitudes to tertiary education/Economic climate/Attitudes to women working/Access and attitudes to childcare facilities/Availability of welfare support, for example, unemployment benefits.

A change in these factors will result in either a shift of the labour curve to the left (decrease in the supply of labour) or right (an increase in the supply of labour), as shown below.

1 Rise in the school leaving age

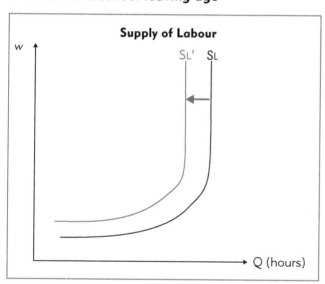

As young people are required to stay at school longer they are no longer available to work at any wage rate. This is a decrease in the supply of labour. The graph shifts left.

2 Compulsory retirement age abandoned

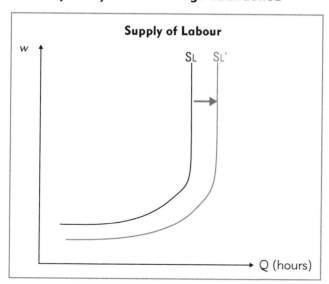

As older people are no longer forced to leave work, more people will be available to work at all wage rates. This is an increase in the supply of labour. The graph shifts right.

ISBN: 9780170215718

1 Copy and complete the diagram below to show the factors that affect the supply of labour.

Examples:

_____

What would affect the SUPPLY OF LABOUR?

Examples:

_____

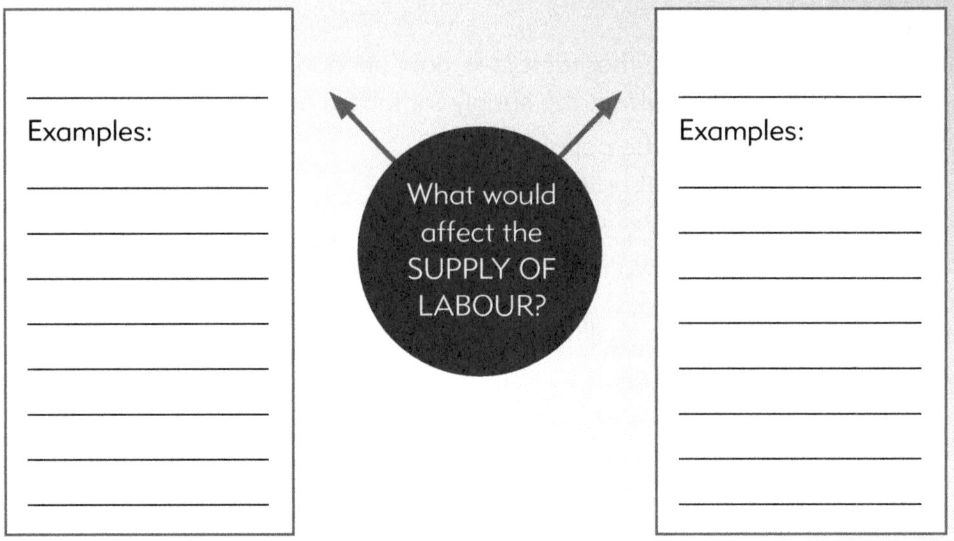

2 Copy and complete the table below.

Scenario	Change in the supply for labour: Increase or decrease?	Shift in the supply of labour curve left or right?	Explanation
a Government lowers school leaving age			
b Massive immigration experienced			
c Childcare subsidies are cut, raising costs of childcare			
d Fall in numbers attending tertiary education institutions			
e Unemployment benefit slashed			
f Change in income tax rates benefiting families with only one working parent			
g New Zealanders emigrate to Australia			
h Compulsory retirement reintroduced			
i School starting age dropped to 3 years			

ISBN: 9780170215718

The labour market

The market diagram below illustrates the interaction of the sellers of labour (supply of labour, i.e. households) and the buyers of labour (demand for labour, i.e. firms).

The **equilibrium wage** (We) rate is *that wage rate where the quantity of labour demanded (available jobs) equals the quantity of people willing to work.* At this wage rate everyone who is willing to work is able to find a job. The market is said to **clear**. This is *not* to say that everyone in the labour force is employed. Those who are not employed are choosing not to be available at this wage rate. They are called the **voluntary unemployed**. As they are not available for work they do not meet any of the criteria for unemployment as defined earlier in Unit 32. At the equilibrium wage rate there is no involuntary unemployment. Everyone willing to work at that wage rate can find a job.

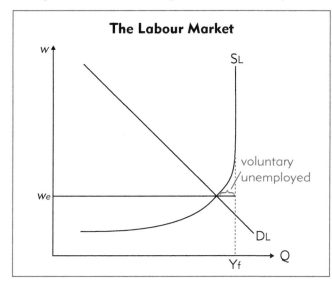

The Labour Market

S_L = the number of workers willing to work at each wage rate.

D_L = the number of jobs available at each wage rate.

w_e = equilibrium wage rate.

Y_f = total quantity of labour available in economy.

ISBN: 9780170215718

ACTIVITY

1 Explain why the voluntary unemployed are 'not really unemployed'.
2 Copy and complete the following table.

Scenario	Affects supply or demand of labour?	Increase or decrease?	Graph (show change)	Effect on wages and employment
a Global economic recession				
b School leaving age falls				
c Increased spending by government on health				

Economics for NCEA Level 2

Scenario	Affects supply or demand of labour?	Increase or decrease?	Graph (show change)	Effect on wages and employment
d Exports fall			w (wages) / Q (hours) S_L D_L	
e Female participation rates rise			w (wages) / Q (hours) S_L D_L	
f Unemployment benefits improved			w (wages) / Q (hours) S_L D_L	
g Increased immigration			w (wages) / Q (hours) S_L D_L	
h Personal income tax rates fall			w (wages) / Q (hours) S_L D_L	
i Increase in tourist numbers to New Zealand			w (wages) / Q (hours) S_L D_L	
j New government reintroduces compulsory retirement			w (wages) / Q (hours) S_L D_L	
k Increased labour productivity			w (wages) / Q (hours) S_L D_L	
l Increased consumer spending			w (wages) / Q (hours) S_L D_L	

ISBN: 9780170215718

5 ▪ Inflexibility in the Labour Market

By the end of this unit you will be able to:
- Use the concept of real wages to explore disequilibrium in the labour market.
- Explain inflexibility in the labour market.
- Outline the different perspectives that different groups bring to wage negotiations.

Wages are the price of labour. There are two measures of wages: nominal and real. Both are used in Economics and there is still considerable debate about the importance of each in explaining labour markets. The difference between them is explored here. The inability of labour markets to clear is also explored in more detail, and the supply and demand model of the labour market is used to illustrate the concepts raised.

Real wages versus nominal wages

Real wages *(w/p)* are the purchasing power of the nominal wage **or** the nominal wage adjusted for inflation. For example, a worker who earned $10 in 1969 would have a higher real wage than a worker who earned $10 in 2004, because the $10 earned in 1969 could buy much more. Inflation has eroded the purchasing power of the wage.

Nominal wages *(w)* are the actual dollar value of the wage. This is what you actually receive in payment; for example, $40 a night babysitting or $15 an hour working at the supermarket.

In general we look at real wages rather than nominal wages for both workers and employers. Workers are more interested in what they can buy as a measure of their well-being and so judge a pay rate not on its nominal value but on its real value. Employers/producers are interested in profit, i.e. the relationship between their costs (wages) to their revenues (prices). Real wages reflect this relationship.

Real wages are indicated by the symbol *w/p* on the vertical axis of a labour market diagram.

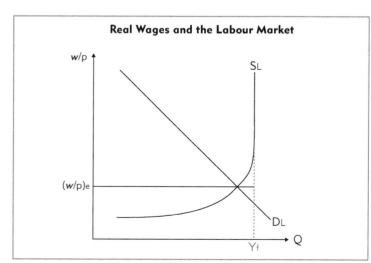

Real Wages and the Labour Market

S_L = those who are willing to work at each wage rate.

D_L = jobs available at each wage rate.

w/p = real wage rate.

Y_f = total quantity of labour available in the economy.

ISBN: 9780170215718

Economics for NCEA Level 2

The equilibrium real wage rate is determined by the intersection of the demand for labour curve and the supply of labour curve (w/p_e). At this real wage rate the market will clear.

If real wages paid are above the w/p equilibrium rate (w/p^l), there will be a surplus of available workers or **involuntarily unemployed** workers – people who are available to work at this wage rate but unable to find a job. There is pressure on real wages to fall. This will involve either a rise in prices or a fall in nominal wage rates. In fact the nominal wage rate in a free labour market would fall as there are surplus workers and firms can lower wages but still secure workers.

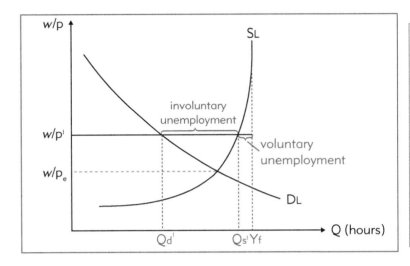

w/p = real wage rate.
w/p_e = equilibrium real wage.
w/p^l = real wage rate above the equilibrium real wage.
Qd^l = quantity of jobs available at the $(w/p)^l$.
Qs^l = quantity of labour willing to work at (w/p).
Y_F = total quantity of labour available in the economy.

If real wage rates paid are below the w/p equilibrium rate, there will be a shortage of available workers. This causes pressure on real wages to rise. This will involve either a fall in prices or a rise in nominal wage rates. In reality the nominal wage rate in a free labour market would rise as there is a shortage of workers, and firms will bid for the available workers by offering more attractive wages.

The existence of involuntary unemployment in New Zealand suggests that the labour market does not clear, i.e. it does not operate at equilibrium. While labour shortages are short-lived — suggesting upward movement of nominal wage rate occurs readily — involuntary unemployment has lingered, suggesting downward movement of nominal wage rates does not occur so readily, a phenomenon known as **sticky wages**.

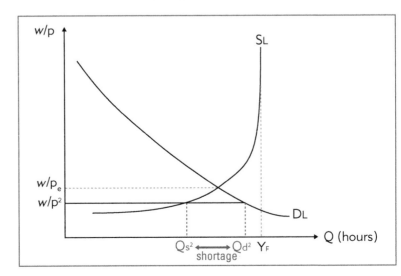

w/p = real wage rate.
w/p_e = equilibrium real wage.
w/p^2 = real wage rate above the equilibrium real wage.
Qs^2 = quantity of labour willing to work at $(w/p)^2$.
Qd^2 = quantity of jobs available at the $(w/p)^2$.
Y_F = total quantity of labour available in the economy.

ISBN: 9780170215718

ACTIVITY

1 Explain what is meant by the term nominal wages.

2 Explain what is meant by the term real wages.

3 Explain the term purchasing power with respect to real wages.

4 Explain why real wages are more important to workers than nominal wages.

Read the resource article below and answer these questions.

5 Define involuntary unemployment.

6 Define voluntary unemployment.

7 Using the labour market model illustrate a labour market with involuntary unemployment.

8 Explain why a labour market may have involuntary unemployment.

9 Identify the reasons why a labour market may not clear.

10 Explain how the labour market differs from a goods and services market.

Why wages do not fall in recessions

From *The Economist* print edition

An intrepid economist ventures into the real world to investigate – and finds conventional explanations wanting

ECONOMISTS dislike talking to people. They prefer a more "scientific" approach to research, such as number-crunching or abstract theorising. But that can be a weakness, as a new book by Truman Bewley, an economist at Yale University, makes clear. In "Why Wages Don't Fall During A Recession", published by Harvard University Press, he tackles one of the oldest, and most controversial, puzzles in economics: why nominal wages rarely fall (and real wages do not fall enough) when unemployment is high. But he does so in a novel way, through interviews with over 300 businessmen, union leaders, job recruiters and unemployment counsellors in the north-eastern United States during the early 1990s recession.

Explanations for why wages are sticky abound, but they are often unconvincing. Neoclassical economists, who have a starry-eyed faith in the efficiency of markets, think wage rigidity is an illusion. In their view, workers quit their jobs when pay starts to fall in a downturn. This stops wages falling much and makes them appear inflexible. But their theory implies that unemployment in a recession is voluntary – a view at which reasonable people might rightly scoff.

Keynesians, who accept that markets are often imperfect, think wages are sticky, but cannot agree why. Some blame unions or established employees ("insiders") for blocking pay cuts. Keynes himself thought that workers were so concerned about their wages relative to those at other firms that no company dared to cut pay. Others argue that firms pay high "efficiency wages" in order to make the threat of job loss more costly for workers and so spur them to work harder. (Wages might still fall in a recession though, since workers are more afraid of not finding another job when unemployment rises.) Still others claim that firms implicitly insure workers against a fall in income in exchange for lower long-term average wages. And so on.

One or more of these theories may be true. Or perhaps none is. Economists do not really know, because the labour-market data with which they test their theories is inadequate. So Mr Bewley tried asking people who should be in the know. He is aware of the pitfalls: interviewees may be unrepresentative, lie or obfuscate. They may not understand their own motives. Still, since economists are ultimately trying to describe human behaviour, meeting real people ought sometimes to help.

Mr Bewley finds scant evidence to support the various wage-stickiness theories.

ISBN: 9780170215718

Economics for NCEA Level 2

His interviewees say unions are not to blame for wage rigidity: few American firms are unionised, and in those where unions are important "the first line of resistance to pay reduction was almost always management." Nor are "insiders" blocking pay cuts: few non-union workers bargain over wages with their employers, and no employer remarked on a sharp division of opinion over layoffs among workers, who more typically thought that pay cuts would not save jobs.

Keynes's theory gets short shrift too. Mr Bewley finds that, although pay rates across non-union companies are connected by supply and demand, firms still have plenty of latitude in setting pay because workers have scant knowledge of pay rates elsewhere. Nor is much credence given to the efficiency-wage model. "People do work harder during a recession because they are concerned about their jobs … however, the logic does not imply that companies pay well for reasons of discipline. They do so in order to attract and retain employees," says a typical personnel officer in a middling manufacturer. The implicit insurance model fares little better. Employers do not think such a bargain exists and believe that it would be unenforceable in any case, since long-term pay is determined by competitive conditions.

All in a day's work

Why, then, are wages sticky? Mr Bewley concludes that employers resist pay cuts largely because the savings from lower wages are usually outweighed by the cost of denting workers' morale: pay cuts hit workers' standard of living and lower their self-esteem. Falling morale raises staff turnover and reduces productivity. Cheerier workers are more productive workers, not only because they work better, but also because they identify more closely with the company's interests. This last point is crucial. Mr Bewley argues that monitoring workers' performance is usually so tricky that firms rarely rely on coercion and financial carrots alone as motivators. In particular, high morale fosters teamwork and information-sharing, which are otherwise difficult to encourage.

Firms typically prefer layoffs to pay cuts because they harm morale less, says Mr Bewley. Pay cuts hurt everybody and can cause festering resentment; layoffs hit morale only for a while, since the aggrieved have, after all, left. And whereas a generalised pay cut might make the best workers leave, and a selective one damage morale because it is seen as unfair, firms can often lay off their least competent staff.

Mr Bewley's theory has some interesting implications. Pay cuts are more likely at firms whose demand for labour is price-sensitive, such as those in highly competitive industries. Since many markets are becoming more competitive, wages may also be getting more flexible – and unemployment may rise less in recessions. Wages are also likely to be less rigid in short-term jobs, where workers do not become attached to their firm. On the other hand, since more workers now do jobs that are hard to monitor, or in which they need to co-operate, share information, be creative or be nice to customers, wages may become stickier.

Mr Bewley's book is not the last word on sticky wages. Some of his findings are probably specific to the north-eastern United States in the early 1990s. But his theory has a ring of truth to it. And if his example spurs other economists to venture out of their ivory towers, so much the better.

ISBN: 9780170215718

Minimum wage

A minimum wage is a price minimum for labour. This means it is illegal to pay below this wage rate.

The supply and demand model for the labour market can be used to illustrate the effect of a minimum wage.

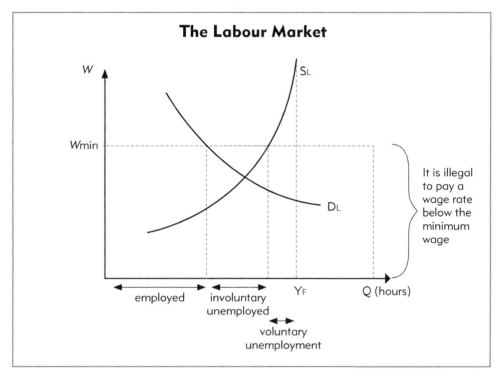

Looking at the model it is clear that, when imposed at a rate above the equilibrium wage rate, a minimum wage will cause wages to rise. It will also lead to increased involuntary unemployment as at equilibrium there is no involuntary unemployment. Minimum wages are used in New Zealand. This is because, despite their impact on involuntary unemployment, the price paid for labour represents a household's ability to live. The rate of pay must be sufficient that a household can meet an acceptable standard of living.

The minimum wage rate must be set above the market equilibrium to have an effect. Any minimum wage rate set below the equilibrium wage rate means the labour market will clear.

ISBN: 9780170215718

Economics for NCEA Level 2

The minimum wage

There are three minimum wage rates:

- The **adult minimum wage** applies to all employees aged 16 and over who are not new entrants or trainees
- The **new entrants minimum wage** applies to employees aged 16 and 17, except for those who have completed 200 hours or three months of employment in the workforce, whichever is shorter; or who are supervising or training other workers; or who are trainees
- The **training minimum wage** applies only to employees aged 16 and over who are doing recognised industry training involving at least 60 credits a year.

There is no statutory minimum wage for employees who are under 16 years old.

A small number of people hold an exemption from the minimum wage.

The minimum wage rates are reviewed every year. As of 1 April 2011 the adult minimum wage rates (before tax) that apply for employees aged 16 or over are:

- $13.00 per hour, which is
    - $104.00 for an 8-hour day or
    - $520.00 for a 40-hour week.

The rates that apply to new entrants, and employees on the training minimum wage (before tax), are:

- $10.40 per hour, which is
    - $83.20 for an 8-hour day or
    - $416.00 for a 40-hour week.

Employees have to be paid at least the minimum hourly wage rate for any extra time worked over eight hours a day or 40 hours a week.

Source: www.dol.govt.nz

ACTIVITY

1 Explain why a wage (the price of labour) is different to the price of a good or service.

2 Compare and contrast possible arguments for and against a minimum wage.

3 Using the supply and demand model illustrate the effect of a minimum wage being introduced in the labour market. Fully explain the impacts on employment and wage rates.

ISBN: 9780170215718

Minimum wage debate rages on

Labour claims a rise in the minimum wage would have a small effect on growth, but the Prime Minister says supporters of the move don't understand economics.

Supporters of an increase in the minimum wage are questioning claims it would hike unemployment but Prime Minister John Key says they don't understand economics.

At Labour's congress at the weekend the party said it would increase the minimum wage from the current $13 an hour to $15.

The Government responded saying Labour Department advice was that it would quickly put 6000 people on the dole because companies would not be able to afford higher wage bills.

Labour leader Phil Goff said the change would have a small impact on growth.

"The point is people have to have a living wage, and people can't live on $13 an hour when prices are sky rocketing."

Green co-leader Metiria Turei said the Labour Department actually said that increasing the minimum wage to $15 an hour could result in a "potential loss in job growth" of 4280-5710 jobs.

"That's very different from putting 6000 people out of work," she said.

"A potential loss in job growth can occur without a solitary person being put out of work.

It all depends on the wider economic policy settings."

The methodology for the figures was questionable and other analysis showed the increase was unlikely to impact on employment, she said.

Unite Union national director Mike Treen said the department talked about job losses that equated to about 0.2 per cent of the labour force.

"That is really margin of error stuff for a workforce of 2.2 million. It is even small compared to the actual job losses of 150,000 over the past three years as a consequence of the economic crisis and failure of the Government to implement policies designed to protect jobs."

In the early 2000s employment rose along with the minimum wage.

Employers had benefitted for years from rising productivity without commensurate wage rises, he said.

Wellington People's Centre's Kay Brereton said taxpayers were subsidising employers paying the minimum wage through the Working for Families Tax Credit package.

"Increasing the minimum wage would put the costs onto the employers who are benefiting from the labour of their employees."

In a speech to a business group near Wellington today, Mr Key defended his rejection of raising the wage. He said the Government decided to grant a raise when it came into office at a time when business was struggling.

"We wanted to do what we thought was fair and that was to make sure that those that earned the least were keeping up with inflation."

However now was not the time to up it again, he said. Increases would result in job losses or higher costs for consumers.

"If anyone thinks we can just magically increase the minimum wage with no implication on either labour markets or costs to employers they don't understand basic economics," he said.

"The way we will lift our wages is to have a very productive environment."

- NZPA

ACTIVITY

1 Explain why John Key believes supporters of minimum wage rate rises do not understand economics.

2 Compare and contrast the difference between the phrases 'potential loss in job growth' and 'job losses'.

3 Explain the comment *'taxpayers were subsidising employers paying the minimum wage through the Working for Families Tax Credit package'.*

4 Compare and contrast the Working for Families tax credit and a minimum wage.

ISBN: 9780170215718

Economics for NCEA Level 2

6 ▪ Types of Unemployment

By the end of this unit you will be able to:
- Define structural, frictional, seasonal and cyclical unemployment.
- Recognise these as forms of involuntary unemployment.
- Explain the pattern of the business cycle and relate it to cyclical unemployment.
- Define and explain the natural rate of unemployment.

Involuntary unemployment

The concept of involuntary unemployment was introduced on page 70. This term covers anyone who is willing to work at the current wage rate but is unable to find a job. The reasons for people being in this predicament are varied. Finding solutions to the unemployment problems faced by these individuals may require quite different responses. This unit expands the idea of involuntary unemployment.

The existence of involuntary unemployed – those who are willing to work at the given wage rate but cannot find a job – can be explained by the following economic concepts:

- **Structural unemployment:** *Unemployment caused by an imbalance between the skills of workers and the requirements of employers.* This is generally caused by falls in final demand for particular goods and services, perhaps because the final good is now obsolete or unpopular, or because there is a permanent technological change, e.g. automation of a factory.
- **Frictional unemployment:** *Short-term unemployment caused by people temporarily between jobs, entering the job market for the first time or changing jobs where there is a few weeks of unemployment before starting the new job.* Frictional unemployment is seen as a sign of a healthy economy — where workers are moving from position to position. **Seasonal unemployment** is unemployment caused by the regular seasonal nature of the work (e.g. ski workers in the snow season, fruit picking in the summer season). Seasonal unemployment is a type of frictional unemployment.
- **Cyclical unemployment:** *Unemployment caused by a downturn in economic activity generally.* The pattern of change in the level of economic activity is known as the **business cycle**. Cyclical unemployment may be the result of inward shifts (or falls in) aggregate demand (see page 35).

ISBN: 9780170215718

The Business Cycle

Economic activity

1 Downturn
2 Trough/
   Recession
3 Upturn/Recovery
4 Peak or boom

trend over time

Time

1 Classify the following examples of structural (S), frictional (F) or cyclical (C) unemployment:
   a A worker involved in fruit picking in Marlborough for six months of the year cannot find another job.
   b A mother trying to return to part-time work after taking time out to raise children.
   c A bank teller laid off following increased Internet banking by customers.
   d A tourism worker laid off following the global economic recession caused by a terrorist attack.
   e A worker in Taranaki made redundant following a firm's decision to relocate to Hamilton.
   f Advertising agency industry workers laid off during a recession.

2 Which type of unemployment should a government target when trying to reduce unemployment levels? Explain why.

3 With reference to types of involuntary unemployment, how do you explain the two pieces of information contained in these newspaper headlines published on the same day?

Shortage of skills cramping growth

The Labour Department Survey in May reported that 39 per cent of businesses are finding it hard to secure the skills they need to expand. And 12 per cent of all businesses rate their inability to find labour as their biggest constraint to boosting output.

Unemployment Rate at 5.4 per cent

4 Explain the difference between cyclical and structural unemployment.

5 Using the Labour Market (supply and demand model), illustrate the effect of an upturn in the business cycle on wage rates, unemployment and employment.

ISBN: 9780170215718

Economics for NCEA Level 2

Economic models and unemployment

AS/AD model

The AS/AD model was introduced in the inflation unit. It shows the relationship between Price Levels and Real Output. The full employment line (Y_F) can be used to show the gap between the output that could be produced at full employment and the level of output currently being produced. The gap between these two output levels can be used to demonstrate the underutilised resources in the economy. That is to say, it shows the unemployed resources of the economy (the unemployed).

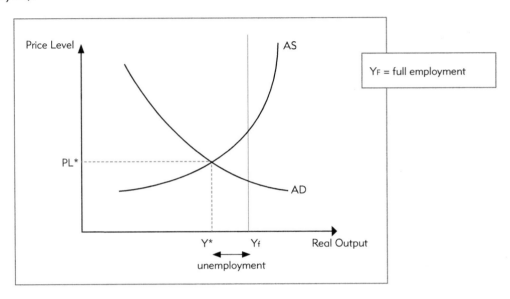

Y_F = full employment

Increased cyclical unemployment may be caused by decreases in AD — a leftward shift of the AD curve. This is called **demand deficient unemployment**.

For example, as households try to increase savings they spend less on goods and services. The demand for final goods falls. This will shift the aggregate demand curve left. This will result in a fall in real output and thus an increase in unemployment.

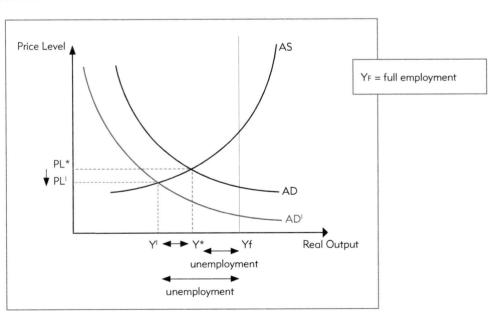

Y_F = full employment

ISBN: 9780170215718

Increased cyclical unemployment may be caused by decreases in AS — a leftward shift of the AS curve. This is called **supply side unemployment**.

For example, the cost of imported raw materials rises. The rise in costs of production causes the AS curve to shift to the left. This will result in a fall in real output and thus an increase in unemployment.

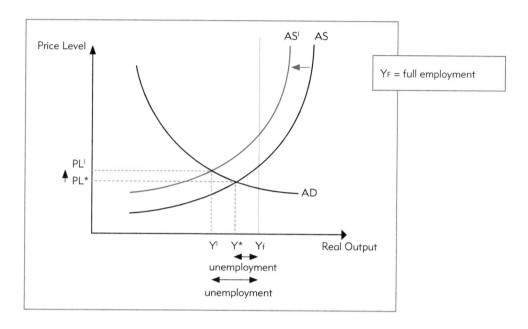

The circular flow model

The circular flow model can also be used to illustrate these changes. This model is useful when analysing the impact on various groups within the economy.

Using the example above, as households try to increase savings they spend less on goods and services. The demand for final goods falls. This will shift the aggregate demand curve left. This will result in a fall in real output and thus an increase in unemployment.

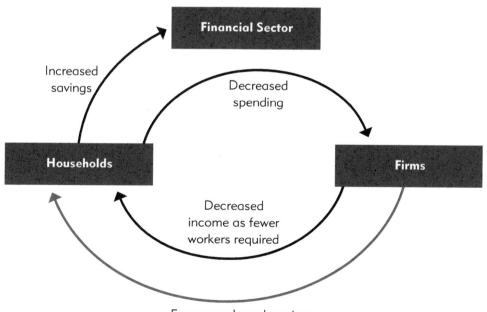

ISBN: 9780170215718

Economics for NCEA Level 2

The Production Possibility Frontier can also be used to illustrate increases in unemployment.

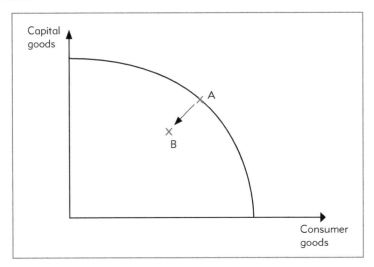

As the economy experiences a downturn, real output falls. This is illustrated as a move away from the frontier towards the origin.

ACTIVITY

1 The world economy has suffered a major economic downturn since the global financial meltdown. New Zealand has experienced a long economic recession.

a Illustrate the effects of this recession on unemployment using the AS/AD model.

b Illustrate the effects of this recession on unemployment using the PPF model.

c Illustrate the effect of this recession on unemployment using the circular flow model.

2 Increased spending by the government to rebuild Christchurch following the earthquake in 2011 has caused increased demand for construction industry workers.

a Illustrate the effect of the increased government spending using the Labour Market model.

b Illustrate the effect of the increased government spending using the circular flow model.

c Illustrate the effect of the increased government spending using the AS/AD model.

ISBN: 9780170215718

Full employment revisited

Economists generally agree that even if an economy were operating at its potential (full utilisation of resources and technology), that is, **full employment**, some unemployment would still exist. This is known as the **natural rate of unemployment**. An economy at full potential must also be, by definition, experiencing no cyclical unemployment. Thus:

natural rate of unemployment = frictional unemployment + structural unemployment

The natural rate of unemployment is hard to determine but economists have made 'guestimates'. For example the so-called Humphrey-Hawkins Act (1978) in the United States set 4% as the government target for unemployment, acknowledging a natural rate of unemployment of 4%. However, many US economists consider 6% more realistic.

ACTIVITY

1 Give three examples of workers whom economists would describe as being 'naturally' unemployed.
2 Why is natural unemployment not counted when considering the concept of full employment as shown on the PPF?
3 In New Zealand's economic boom period, unemployment fell to approximately 3%. Explain why the labour market did not clear. Refer to the national rate of unemployment and the different types of unemployment in your answer.

ISBN: 9780170215718

7 ▪ The Impacts of Unemployment

By the end of this unit you will be able to:
- Explore the economic and social effects of unemployment.
- Explain the impact of changes in unemployment on various groups in New Zealand society.

There are two main reasons for worrying about unemployment. Economically it results in reduced output, and socially it produces human suffering. If you happen to be a politician you may feel unemployment has a political effect as well. It is one of the economic statistics that receives widespread publicity, and because of its 'people aspect' governments are judged on it. We will study both the economic and social effects of unemployment.

Economic effects of unemployment

The circular flow model can be used to illustrate some of the economic effects of unemployment.

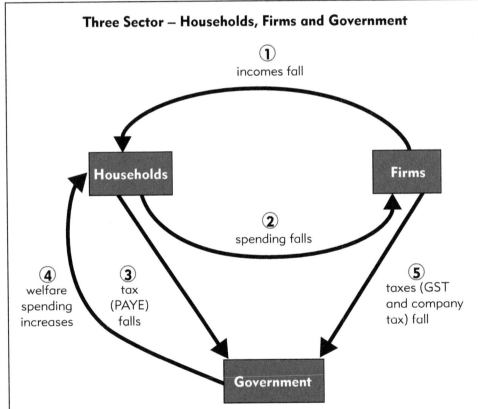

Three Sector – Households, Firms and Government

① incomes fall

Households

Firms

② spending falls

④ welfare spending increases

③ tax (PAYE) falls

⑤ taxes (GST and company tax) fall

Government

Effects

① The income levels of households fall as less of the resource 'labour' is being sold to firms.

② With less income there is less demand for goods and services so production will fall.

These reactions can continue to spiral.

The government (which taxes workers and transfers part of this income to the unemployed) will experience:

③ a decrease in tax take but …
④ an increase in welfare spending on unemployment benefits.

The tax take is further reduced through the fall in consumer spending which:

⑤ will reduce GST collection.

With the reduction in income levels there will be a fall in the level of savings, which will have a flow-on effect to lower the availability of investment funds.

As the duration of unemployment lengthens – the time spent unemployed – the loss of skills increases. This is a loss of human capital. Efforts put in to increasing an individual's skills and training are eroded the longer a person is

ISBN: 9780170215718

unemployed. In New Zealand, where training is subsidised by the state, this is a further cost to the taxpayer.

In summary the economic effects of unemployment are:

- **decreased production levels**
- **decreased income levels**
- **increased social welfare spending**
- **reduced tax take**
- **decreased savings**
- **decreased investment levels**
- **a loss of skills or a decrease in human capital.**

Social effects of unemployment

Unemployment and social stress

Although difficult to quantify (measure), the reason unemployment is such a highly charged issue is the human suffering that usually accompanies it. In addition to the loss of income and skills outlined above, the unemployed experience a loss of self-esteem, low morale, frustration and boredom. The stress within a household for all members, not only the person unemployed, can be extreme. Obviously the longer the unemployment continues the greater these effects become. These effects can also produce physical health issues.

Unemployment and migration

The economic idea of resource use is that production processes that are not efficient and sustainable will fail, and the resources used by these firms will move to other processes where they will be used more efficiently. This assumes perfect mobility of resources. Mobility of resources refers to the ability of a resource to move or adapt. Geographical mobility refers to the ability of a resource, in this case labour, to move from one physical location to another. Occupational mobility refers to the ability of a resource, in this case labour, to move from one production process to another. However labour is far from perfectly mobile.

- **Geographical mobility** is often affected by social factors, for instance a parent's desire to remain in an area for the education available, the commitment to a stable family life for children, a partner who is also working and committed to a job, wider family ties to an area, or lifestyle choices overriding employment issues.
- **Occupational mobility** may be affected by the skill levels of the worker — higher skill levels are generally regarded as more mobile. This is especially true of international mobility where the destination country may have skill requirements for migrants.

ISBN: 9780170215718

Economics for NCEA Level 2

Unemployment and inequality

A previous unit highlighted the fact that unemployment does not strike equally across all members of an economy. Thus the damaging economic and social effects are not felt evenly across the economy.

Who are the Unemployed?

| % represent unemployment rates |

154,000 June qtr 2011

Educational characteristics

No qualifications	9.4%
School qualifications	8.3%
Tertiary below bachelors	5.8%
Bachelors degree or higher	4.1%

Ethnicity

European	4.7%
Maori	13.7%
Pacific peoples	13.1%
Asian	12.1%
Other ethnicities	4.7%

Age

15-19 years	27.6%
20-24 years	11.2%
25-29 years	5.9%
30-34 years	4.8%
35-39 years	4.5%
40-44 years	5.3%
45-49 years	4.6%
50-54 years	2.9%
55-59 years	3.6%
60-64 years	3.0%
65+ years	1.8%

Regional distribution

Northland	7.3%
Auckland	7.3%
Waikato	6.5%
Bay of Plenty	6.9%
Gisborne/Hawke's Bay	7.2%
Taranaki/Wanganui	6.9%
Manawatu/Wanganui	6.9%
Wellington	5.5%
Tasman/Marlborough	5.5%
West Coast Regions	4.4%
Canterbury Region	5.7%
Otago	5.3%
Southland	3.4%

Gender

Female unemployment rate is 6.6%

Male unemployment rate is 6.5%

ISBN: 9780170215718

1

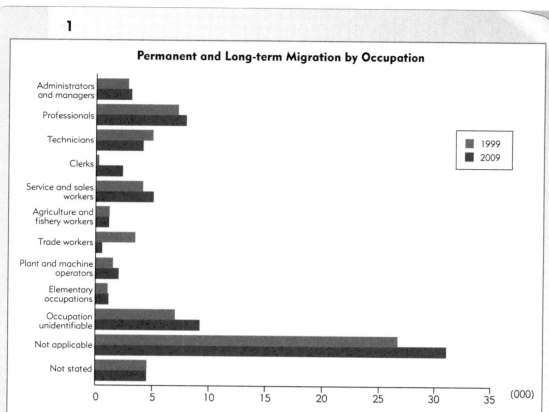

Permanent and Long-term Migration by Occupation

Legend: 1999, 2009

Occupations (y-axis):
- Administrators and managers
- Professionals
- Technicians
- Clerks
- Service and sales workers
- Agriculture and fishery workers
- Trade workers
- Plant and machine operators
- Elementary occupations
- Occupation unidentifiable
- Not applicable
- Not stated

x-axis: 0, 5, 10, 15, 20, 25, 30, 35 (000)

Using the graph on occupation migration above:

  a Identify occupations (workers) you consider to have high geographical mobility.

  b Identify occupations (workers) you consider to have low geographical mobility.

2 With reference to the statistics on the previous page, justify your answers to **a** and **b** above.

3 Using the information in this unit, copy and complete this summary diagram.

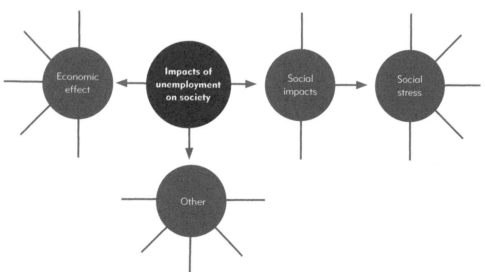

Economic effect — Impacts of unemployment on society — Social impacts — Social stress — Other

4 Explain how unemployment affects different groups in New Zealand differently. Use the data provided on page 84 to support your answer.

ISBN: 9780170215718

ISBN: 9780170215718

Economics for NCEA Level 2

8 ▪ The Government and Unemployment

By the end of this unit you will be able to:
- Understand how government policy can alleviate the causes of unemployment.
- Explore the potential for institutional change in the labour market.
- Explain the effect on employment of government spending, taxation (fiscal policy) and trade restrictions.

Achieving low levels of unemployment is important to any government. In times of relatively low unemployment it may not appear to be a priority. Since the mid-1980s, when New Zealand's unemployment was very high, institutional changes have been the primary focus of government policy. Institutional changes refer to changes in the labour market itself. The aim of these changes was increased flexibility and productivity leading to lower costs and increased employment (and growth). One major change was the introduction of the 1991 Employment Contracts Act. This Act was replaced by the Employment Relations Act 2000. Fiscal policy has been used primarily to target the effects of unemployment but there have also been government initiatives to reduce unemployment. Most significant of these is the Working For Families package, announced in the 2004 Budget. Changes did not take effect until 2005.

Since then other significant changes have included the four week annual paid holiday entitlement, introduced in 2007, raising the number of holiday weeks from three to four.

In 2008 a 90-day trial period for new employees was introduced. The aim was to try and encourage reluctant employers — fearful of being unable to reduce the number of employees at a later date — to take someone on in a trial capacity. No reason for dismissal within the 90-day period is required. The trial was deemed successful and the 90-day scheme widened to all producers in 2011.

In 2011 employees gained the legal right to cash in their fourth week of annual leave.

Deregulation of the labour market

As with most areas of the New Zealand economy, the post World War Two labour market became increasingly regulated. Trade unions were widespread and at times membership was compulsory. Most wage rates were dominated by national awards that were negotiated on behalf of workers by national trade unions. The 1991 ECA (Employment Contracts Act) was designed to remove power from the national trade unions and put a stop to collective bargaining, as it was then known. This was an attempt to improve labour market flexibility. Negotiations were to be site specific. Collective site agreements were permitted under the Act and, although it was envisioned that individual contracts (no collective bargaining at all) would be the norm, in fact collective contracts were widespread. Minimum standards are still required by law and can not be negotiated away, e.g. holiday requirements of the 1981 Holidays Act.

The Employment Relations Act (ERA), introduced by a newly elected Labour Government in 2000, was seen by employer groups as a step backwards because it reinstated 'good faith' bargaining and encouraged collective bargaining. However some of the fears expressed prior to the enactment of the law have been largely unrealised.

The most significant change in the labour market since the ERA has been the 90-day trial period for new employees.

90-day employment bill passed

Last updated 20:44 23/11/2010

BILL PASSES: The 90-day trial period for new employees has been extended to all businesses.

Employment law changes which were fiercely fought by unions and the Labour Party have been passed by Parliament.

The 90-day trial period for new employees has been extended to all businesses, and workers will be able to cash in the fourth week of their annual leave.

The separate bills passed their third readings today, both on votes of 64 to 56.

Labour Minister Kate Wilkinson said the 90-day trial period, which previously applied to businesses with 20 or fewer employees, had been a success.

It was introduced soon after the 2008 election, amid strident union protest.

"Rather than have the sky falling in, as was hysterically proclaimed, employers of small and medium-sized businesses gained the confidence to hire new employees," Ms Wilkinson said.

"It is a fact that without the trial period, hundreds of New Zealand workers would not have the jobs they currently do have."

Ms Wilkinson said employers wanted to invest and grow their businesses but didn't want to face a personal grievance if they hired someone who turned out to be unsuitable.

"They simply chose not to hire anyone. The 90-day trial has changed that."

Labour MP Trevor Mallard, the party's labour relations spokesman, said extending the trial period was "just a continuation of the National Party's attack on the rights of wage and salary earners and their conditions".

It would not help the economy and was being done for political and ideological reasons, he said.

"It weakens the processes around job security, extends the range of reasons for dismissal, restricts substantially the right to appeal, and restricts the right to reinstatement," Mr Mallard said.

"This sort of attack drives down wages, it is a tool they are using."

Ms Wilkinson said the law change allowing employees to cash in their fourth week of leave would give them greater choice and flexibility.

"It is incredibly popular and I'm sure the public is very much looking forward to utilising it," she said.

"It is abundantly clear that only the employee can make this request — if an employer does so they will be in breach of the Act."

Under the law change, employees can ask to cash in their fourth week of leave and employers must consider request within a reasonable time.

Employers don't have to agree, and don't have to give a reason for turning it down.

Labour MP Darien Fenton said it had taken unions 30 years to get a fourth week of annual leave.

"We got it in 2003, Australia had it in 1974," she said.

"The Government is advocating for longer hours at work ... over time, it won't be a fourth week of leave, it will be part of salary and we will have lost it."

Another controversial measure in the bill is that it allows employers to ask for proof of illness after the first day of sick leave.

ISBN: 9780170215718

Ms Wilkinson said it would be used "very sparingly" and employers would have to pay for the proof.

"It is clear they will only request a medical certificate when they genuinely suspect someone of routinely pulling sickies," she said.

Ms Fenton said it was a stupid law change.

"No one asked for it, as far as we can tell," she said.

"We don't have a problem with sick leave, the problem is people going to work when they're ill."

National, ACT and United Future supported the bills. Labour, the Greens, the Maori Party and the Progressive Party opposed them.

The changes in both bills come into effect on April 1 next year.

- NZPA

ACTIVITY

Read the newspaper article above.

1 Explain how the 90-day trial law will affect the labour market.

2 Use the Labour Market model to illustrate your answer to 1 above.

3 Explain why employers may support this law.

4 Explain why trade unions and workers may not support this law.

5 Use the article on page 75 to explain why employers are unlikely to take advantage of the new law to implement rapid short-term hiring policies in their workplaces.

Fiscal policy

The term **fiscal** refers to government revenue (taxation) and expenditure (spending). The government's fiscal policy is their intention regarding revenue and expenditure.

> **Operating balance:**
> Taxation – Government Spending (including transfer payments but excluding government spending on capital items).

In response to New Zealand's huge government debt of the 1980s, which was caused by the Think Big projects (designed to boost employment through government spending), the Fiscal Responsibility Act was passed in 1994. The Treasury Department published this explanation of the Fiscal Responsibility Act (FRA):

> The Fiscal Responsibility Act 1994 provides the legislative framework for the conduct of fiscal policy in New Zealand. It aims to improve fiscal policy by establishing five principles of responsible fiscal management and by strengthening the reporting requirements on the Crown. The Act encourages better decision-making by government, strengthens accountability, and ensures more informed public debate about fiscal policy.
>
> Governments are now required to be very transparent about their short- and long-term fiscal intentions. The Act also imposes high standards of financial disclosure on the Crown. The parliament and public of New Zealand now have more financial information about the position of the government, and the risks surrounding that position, than shareholders of most publicly-listed companies.

ISBN: 9780170215718

The FRA sets out to do five things:

- Increase the transparency of policy intentions and the economic and fiscal consequences of government policy.
- Bring a long-term (as well as an annual) focus to budgeting.
- Disclose the aggregate impact of a Budget in advance of the detailed annual budget allocations.
- Ensure independent assessment and reporting of fiscal policy.
- Facilitate parliamentary and public scrutiny of economic and fiscal information and plans.

Part of the motivation for the Act was to address New Zealand's history of poor fiscal performance, to reduce public debt (see the graph below), and to improve fiscal management.

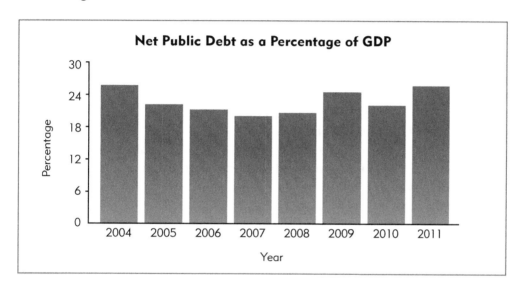

In short, the Fiscal Responsibility Act brought government spending under control. A government is still permitted to run a deficit (spending is greater than taxation income), but repaying the debt incurred by a deficit must be planned for. Debt must be maintained at a *prudent (sensible) level*.

ISBN: 9780170215718

ACTIVITY

1 Define the term fiscal.
2 With reference to the graph above, describe New Zealand's history of fiscal management.
3 Explain the term prudent level of debt.
4 Explain the long-term consequences of debt.
5 Describe the impact of the global financial crisis (2008) and the Christchurch earthquakes (2010 and 2011) on the government's fiscal policy.
6 Explain the difference between a tight/contractionary fiscal policy and a loose/expansionary fiscal policy.
7 Illustrate the effect of an expansionary fiscal policy on output, price level and employment using the AS/AD model. Fully explain the changes.

Economics for NCEA Level 2

Fiscal policy and employment

Historically, the New Zealand labour market has been inflexible, that is, unable to adapt to changing conditions. The inflexibility is caused by the supply of labour being unable to adjust to changes in demand. The reasons for this have in the past included:

- A relatively low average level of skills.
- Workers' reluctance to move from one geographical area to another to follow jobs.
- Historically strong union power.
- National award negotiation.
- 'Us and them' mentality of management and workers.
- Government regulation of industry.
- Inefficient tax system, including high tax rates in the PAYE system.

Part of the government's current fiscal policy is aimed at lowering unemployment rates through increasing flexibility in the labour market. Several areas are targeted.

The Working For Families (WFF) package

The WFF changes were implemented by the Ministry of Social Development (MSD) and Inland Revenue Department (IRD) between October 2004 and April 2007. The objectives of WFF are to:

- Make work pay by supporting families with dependent children so that they are rewarded for their work effort.
- Ensure income adequacy, with a focus on low and middle income families with dependent children to address issues of poverty, especially child poverty.
- Achieve a social assistance system that supports people into work, by making sure that people get the assistance they are entitled to, when they should, and with delivery that supports them into, and to remain in, employment.

Working For Families is a package designed to help make it easier to work and raise a family. It pays extra money to many thousands of New Zealand families. Greater financial support is available for:

- Almost all families with children, earning under $70 000 a year.
- Many families with children, earning up to $100 000 a year.
- Some larger families earning more.

This increased assistance is delivered by Work and Income and Inland Revenue. Working For Families Tax Credits are made up of four types of payments:

- Family tax credit.
- In-work tax credit.
- Minimum family tax credit.
- Parental tax credit.

However, it is an additional payment to workers with families. This means incomes (wages) are higher when the credits are calculated.

ISBN: 9780170215718

Government spending on education

Increased spending in these areas:

- Curriculum review — making subjects more applicable to the needs of employers.
- Assessment review — introduction of NCEA and acknowledging a greater range of skills.
- Subsidised work schemes and training.

Government spending on regional development

High unemployment regions are also low growth regions — initiatives to bolster growth in turn will improve employment.

Government spending on investment in infrastructure

Providing a suitable environment for businesses to perform and grow will improve employment prospects.

Taxation

The other part of fiscal policy is taxation. Taxation is a double-edged sword because while increased taxation allows greater government spending on employment issues it is a cost to producers, and thus acts as a brake on their efforts to grow and employ more people.

Trade restrictions

The effect of trade restrictions and industry protection is covered in the next section. In protecting an industry the government is effectively protecting the jobs of the workers in that industry, too. A policy of free trade (or no trade restrictions) will mean jobs may be lost if goods are purchased more cheaply from overseas (and not produced in this country). However, free trade will boost other sectors of the economy so employment should rise.

ACTIVITY

1 Summarise government initiatives to reduce unemployment levels in a star diagram.

2 Identify any other steps you believe would be effective in solving unemployment.

3 Illustrate the effect of a tight fiscal policy on output, price level and employment using the AS/AD model. Fully explain the changes.

ISBN: 9780170215718

Trade

1 ▪ What is Trade and Why Do It?

By the end of this unit you will be able to:

- Understand the reasons for trade.
- Distinguish between the trade in goods and the trade in services.
- Identify examples of international trade in goods and services.
- Distinguish between onshore and offshore services.
- Outline New Zealand's current trade patterns.

Trade is the exchange of goods (**tangible commodities**) and services (**intangible commodities** or actions performed for someone). Trade occurs everywhere. It can occur between regions within a country (**regional trade**) or between different countries (**international trade**). Economics is the study of how consumers satisfy their **unlimited wants** using their **limited resources**. Each individual, region or country has specific resources at their disposal (**factor endowments**). As in all aspects of life, people play to their strengths, that is, concentrate on what

they are good at. In Economics this is known as **specialisation**. Specialisation can create **surpluses** that can then be traded for the goods and services we have not produced ourselves.

International trade in goods

Throughout the world, different countries have different factor endowments. Australia is rich in minerals and metal ores whereas New Zealand has few easily accessible mineral resources. New Zealand has fertile soil with substantial water resources whereas Saharan Africa does not.

ISBN: 9780170215718

Because New Zealand has excellent growing conditions, New Zealand exports largely agricultural products. Because the country has few minerals or ores, some of our export revenues are directed at importing these products.

New Zealand

Exports — key points	Imports — key point
• A significant reliance on agricultural products. • A significant reliance on a few major markets. • Small manufacturing of high-value products.	• A significant reliance on processed, high-value, manufactured products.

The difference between the types of goods New Zealand exports and imports highlights the weakness in New Zealand's trading position — selling low-value products and buying high-value products.

International trade in services

New Zealand's trade in services has grown significantly since the late 1980s. This growth has seen the range of services imported and exported increase. These services are classified in the following 11 main categories:

- Transportation
- Travel
- Communication services
- Construction services
- Insurance services
- Financial services
- Computer and information services
- Royalties and licence fees
- Other business services
- Personal, cultural and recreational services
- Government services.

Transportation and travel are the two largest service categories. The other nine categories are often grouped together and referred to as 'other services'.

Onshore and offshore services

Services that are traded internationally are classified as **onshore** and **offshore**.

Onshore services are services sold to overseas users but consumed or used within New Zealand. The easiest one to understand is tourism: the users of New Zealand's tourist attractions come from overseas but use hotel rooms, restaurants, adventure rides and so on within New Zealand.

Offshore services are services sold to overseas users that are consumed or used outside of New Zealand, for instance, Air New Zealand transporting foreign passengers between London and Hong Kong.

ISBN: 9780170215718

1 Define the terms:
   a Onshore service.
   b Offshore service.

2 Classify the following as either an onshore or offshore service, or neither.

	Examples
a	Overseas tourists travelling on the interislander ferry service.
b	Australians flying to New Zealand on Qantas.
c	Korean tourists travelling to Otorohonga to see the Kiwihouse.
d	Aucklanders using the Polynesian pools in Rotorua.
e	Foreign freight aboard a ship registered in Liberia insured with a New Zealand maritime insurance agency.
f	British passengers aboard Air New Zealand going to Los Angeles.
g	The Barmy Army hiring New Zealand campervans to follow England in the Rugby World Cup 2011.
h	New Zealanders flying Virgin Blue to Fiji.

What goods do we trade?

	Year ended June		
	2008	2009	2010
Exports by commodity[1]	$ (million)		
Milk powder, butter and cheese	7785	9196	8115
Meat and edible offal	4404	5189	5098
Wood	2096	2193	2354
Crude oil	1586	2555	1875
Mechanical machinery and equipment	1899	1876	1651
Fruit	1295	1477	1604
Fish, crustaceans and molluscs	1107	1251	1229
Aluminium and articles thereof	1477	1392	919
All merchandise exports[2]	**37 156**	**42 989**	**39 657**
Imports by commodity[3]	$ (million)		
Petroleum and products	6005	8525	5806
Mechanical machinery and equipment	5442	6164	4920
Vehicles, parts and accessories	8180	4943	3215
Electricial machinery and equipment	3745	4022	3891
Textiles and textile articles	1900	1973	1908
Plastic and plastic articles	1564	1714	1481
Optical, medical and measuring equipment	1145	1314	1350
All merchandise imports[2]	**41 954**	**48 394**	**39 833**

1 Free on board, including re-exports. (The value of goods at New Zealand ports before export.)
2 Includes commodities not listed.
3 Cost of goods, including insurance and freight to New Zealand.

ISBN: 9780170215718

Who do we trade with?

	Year ended June		
	2008	**2009**	**2010**
Exports	**$ (million)**		
Australia	8205	9928	9221
People's Republic of China	1970	2686	3711
United States of America	4182	4549	3738
Japan	3323	3663	2787
United Kingdom	1636	1699	1680
Korea, Republic of	1362	1294	1255
EU (excluding UK)	1636	4158	3723
All merchandise exports	**37156**	**42989**	**39657**
Imports	**$ (million)**		
Australia	8588	8663	7442
China, People's Republic of	5657	6457	6037
United States of America	3860	4629	4305
Japan	3992	3927	2845
Germany	1980	2069	1636
Singapore	2199	2224	1522
All merchandise imports	**41954**	**48394**	**39833**

ACTIVITY

Using both the current statistics in this unit and the historical data below, explain how successful New Zealand has been in diversifying both markets and export products over time.

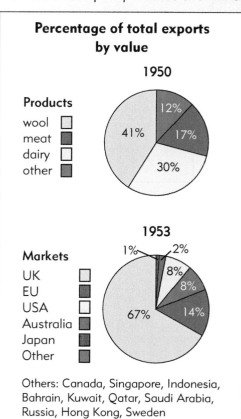

Percentage of total exports by value

1950

Products
wool
meat
dairy
other

12%
17%
30%
41%

1953

Markets
UK
EU
USA
Australia
Japan
Other

1% 2%
8%
8%
67% 14%

Others: Canada, Singapore, Indonesia, Bahrain, Kuwait, Qatar, Saudi Arabia, Russia, Hong Kong, Sweden

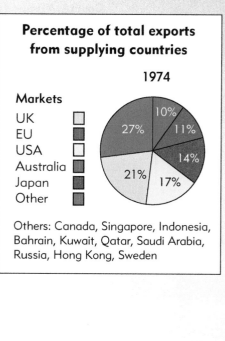

Percentage of total exports from supplying countries

1974

Markets
UK
EU
USA
Australia
Japan
Other

10%
27% 11%
14%
21% 17%

Others: Canada, Singapore, Indonesia, Bahrain, Kuwait, Qatar, Saudi Arabia, Russia, Hong Kong, Sweden

ISBN: 9780170215718

2 ▪ An Economic Model for Trade

By the end of this unit you will be able to:

- Demonstrate, using supply and demand, the basis for trade.
- Explain how world prices, costs of production, and domestic demand determine the quantities imported and exported.
- Explain how factor endowment and technology affect the cost of production.
- Identify influences on demand.

The supply and demand model can be used to illustrate trade between countries. It can be used to show the situation faced by large trading nations and smaller 'price taker' nations. The effects of changes in international conditions can be easily demonstrated using shifts of the supply and demand curves.

The supply and demand model

There are two basic trade scenarios that can be illustrated using the supply and demand model.

SCENARIO ONE — The two-country model
This model is used where the trading countries are able to influence the world price of the commodity.

> We have made some assumptions (simplifications) here:
> - No transport costs.
> - Only two countries trade t[...] good.
> - The prices on each of the axes are the same curren[...] to avoid difficulties with exchange rate variations.

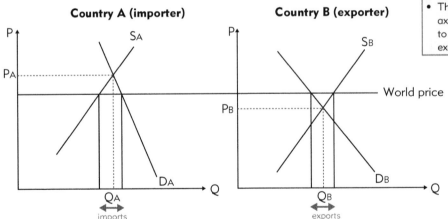

Before trade
Country A: operated at P_A and bought and sold Q_A.
Country B: operated at P_B and bought and sold Q_B.
Clearly if trade is allowed to occur, Country A's consumers would prefer to buy from the cheaper Country B and Country B producers would prefer to sell to the higher-paying Country A. Thus A will import and B will export.

After trade
The supply in Country A increases, as imported goods are supplied and this causes the price in Country A to fall. In Country B the supply decreases, as some produce has been sent overseas. This causes the price in Country B to rise. The prices in the two countries will eventually be the same and there will be no incentive to import or export further goods. This price level is not halfway between the existing prices, rather it is where the quantity exported from B equals the quantity imported to A.

ISBN: 9780170215718

In the model on the previous page we saw that the world price (the traded price) is influenced by the supply of the exports to, and the demand for imports from, the world market. This is not an entirely accurate scenario for many of New Zealand's exports. New Zealand is such a small country that it has no influence on the world price. The quantities we supply and demand from the world are so small that they do not influence the price. New Zealand is a **price-taker**. Irrespective of the quantity imported or exported the world price will not change. We draw the world price as a horizontal line reflecting that the price is constant over all relevant quantities.

A more accurate picture of our trade is shown below.

SCENARIO TWO — The price-taker model

Where the trading countries are **unable** to influence the world price of the commodity. The countries respond to the world price but are unable to change it.

Option 1
World Price > Domestic Price (PA)

Option 2
World Price < Domestic Price (PA)

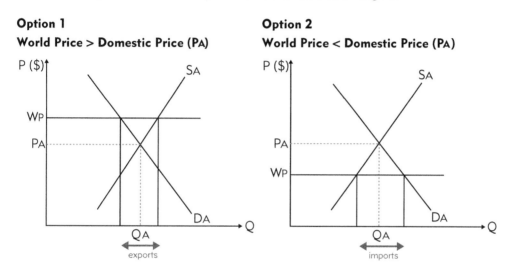

In this scenario the quantities exported and imported can be identified but the 'before-trade price' and the resultant 'after-trade price' is unchanged at WP.

The influences on the quantities imported and exported

SCENARIO ONE — Two-country model

Looking at the scenario on page 96, the quantities imported and exported were determined by the supply and demand in each of the countries. Thus anything that will affect the supply or demand in either country will affect the level of imports and exports.

Demand is affected by:
- Income.
- Tastes and preference.
- Price of related goods (i.e. substitutes and complements).

Supply is affected by:
- Costs of production.
- Technology.
- Price of other goods the producer could make.

These factors can influence either the domestic demand and supply or the overseas demand and supply.

ISBN: 9780170215718

Economics for NCEA Level 2

ISBN: 9780170215718

CASE STUDY

China's demand for meat

China's economy has grown rapidly. The article below shows one of the changes having an impact on New Zealand exports.

Increasing affluence, coupled with a growing appetite for time-saving processed food, is driving the demand for more processed meat meals. Between 2000 and 2008, demand for processed meat products rocketed 345% leading it to become the fastest growing sector within the processed food industry.

Chinese demand for meat drives food processing growth

Editor | Aug 19, 2010

Rising demand for meat will drive the Chinese food processing industry to record double digit growth, according to FoodProductionDaily.com.

Citing market research organization RNCOS's report, Chinese Processed Food Market Analysis, the report said that the Chinese processed food industry will grow at a compound annual growth rate (CAGR) of 33% over the next three years. The processed meat sector is expected to grow at a CAGR of 16% from 2010–2013.

Increasing affluence, coupled with a growing appetite for time-saving processed food is driving the demand for more processed meat meals.

Between 2000 and 2008, demand for processed meat products rocketed 345% leading it to become the fastest growing sector within the processed food industry.

The report also revealed that Chinese consumers are increasingly prepared to accept more low-temperature food products compared with high-temperature food products. This reflects a growing perception of the taste and health benefits of low-temperature foods, according to the report. This trend is already leading major Chinese processed meat manufacturers to boost their production of low-temperature food products.

"We have also found that the availability of processed foods products will improve as modern food-retailing formats look beyond to Tier-1 cities and expand their operation into Tier-2, 3 and rural cities to meet the rising demand from more affluent

consumers," said the researchers. "In order to exploit the opportunities, many local processed food producers have already started focusing on making processed food for domestic sales."

The report also analyses growth factors such as Chinese consumer diet preferences, growing food safety concerns and intensive marketing of processed meat products and processed meat imports and prominent market players.

After processed meat, dairy and ready meals are predicted to be the two highest growing segments in China.

Researchers said the global economic crisis had hardly any impact on the Chinese processed food market.

Source: www.nzexporter.co.nz

ISBN: 9780170215718

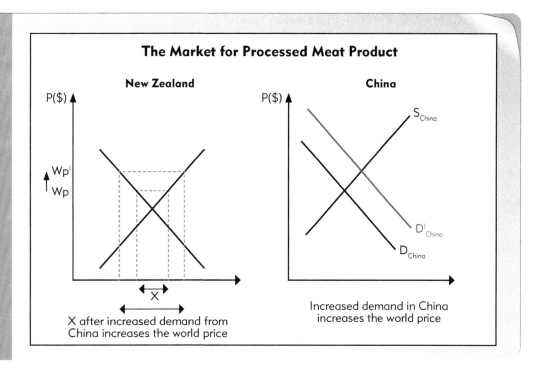

The Market for Processed Meat Product

New Zealand

China

X after increased demand from China increases the world price

Increased demand in China increases the world price

Russia's wheat supply

The Russian grain shortage of 2010 resulted in increases in the world price of wheatflour to consumers. Russia, one of the world's largest exporters of wheat, has banned exports. This will force the world price for wheat to rise, which will have an impact on New Zealand wheat exports.

The Market for New Zealand Wheat (Exports)

After Russia bans wheat exports

X after Russia bans wheat exports

Economics for NCEA Level 2

SCENARIO TWO — Price-taker model

While changes in domestic demand and supply will influence the level of our imports or exports, changes in the demand and supply of our trading partners will only affect imports and exports if they are able to influence the world price. Price-takers respond only to changes in the world price.

Examples:

Factors beyond New Zealand's control have caused the world price of butter to rise. This will lead to a rise in the quantity exported. In New Zealand the price of this product rises to the world price and, while less is consumed by New Zealanders, more is produced domestically.

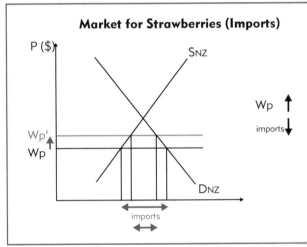

Factors beyond New Zealand's control have caused the world price for strawberries to rise. This will lead to a fall in the quantity imported. In New Zealand the price of this product rises to the world price and, while less is consumed by New Zealanders, domestic production of this good rises.

1 Copy the graphs shown below.

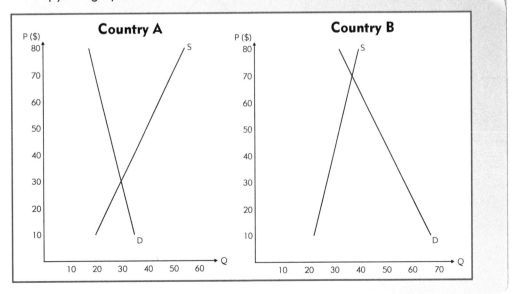

ISBN: 9780170215718

ISBN: 9780170215718

ACTIVITY

a Identify the world price on your graphs, labelling it Wp.

b Identify the quantities exported and imported, labelling them X and M respectively.

c Show how an increase in productivity in Country B would affect:
  i The world price.
  ii The quantity imported and exported.

d Give a detailed explanation of the change(s) you made in **c** above.

2 Copy the graphs shown below.

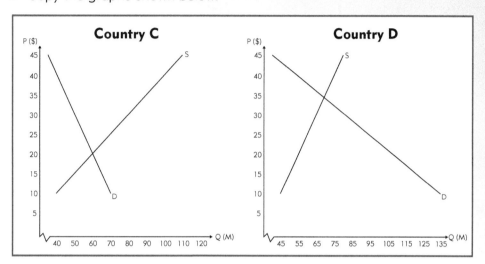

a Identify the world price on your graphs, labelling it Wp.

b Identify the quantities exported and imported, labelling them X and M respectively.

c Show how an increase in incomes in Country C would affect:
  i The world price.
  ii The quantity imported and exported.

d Give a detailed explanation of the change(s) you made in **c** above.

3 Copy the graph shown below.

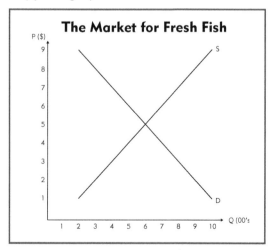

a Show the world price of $7 on your graph.

b Identify the quantity imported or exported, and label appropriately.

c Show how a fall in domestic production of fish following the 2011 tsunami in Japan would affect this market.

d Give a detailed explanation of the change(s) you made in **c** above.

4 Copy the graph shown below.

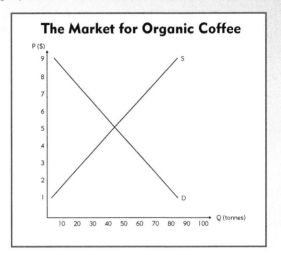

The Market for Organic Coffee

a Show the world price of $3 on your graph.

b Identify the quantity imported or exported, and label appropriately.

c Show how a growing consumer appreciation of the health benefits of organic coffee production methods would affect this market.

d Give a detailed explanation of the change(s) you made in **c** above.

Costs of production vary from country to country because of different factor endowments.

New Zealand's kind of climate means that livestock are not housed indoors in the winter; also grass is, by and large, available all year round. This makes our costs lower than those of northern Europe where animals must be housed and fed grain supplements over the winter months. Also, the level of **technology** affects the costs of production. Improvements in technology produce productivity gains and thus lower the costs of production.

ISBN: 9780170215718

The impacts of changes in trade

Changes in imports and exports affect production levels in New Zealand.

Using our circular flow model we can see that each change has flow-on effects to other groups within the economy.

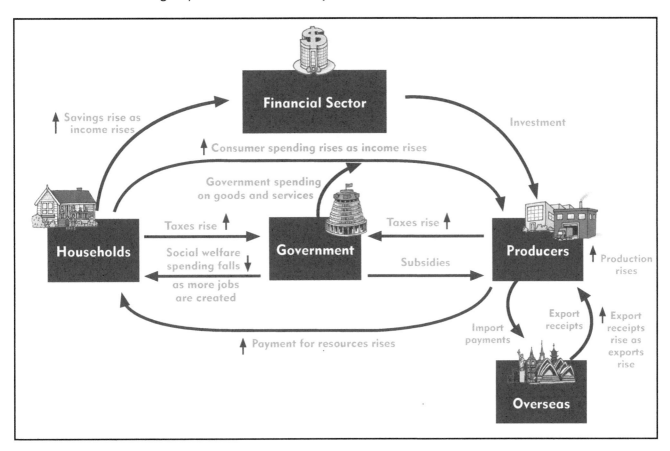

If exports rise (this is an injection into the circular flow) then producers will need to increase production. They will increase their revenues as sales increase.

- More jobs will be created and/or wages will rise to meet this increase in production.
- Households will experience rising incomes.
- Households will increase their spending and/or savings as incomes rise.
- The government will receive more tax and decrease spending on social welfare, e.g. unemployment benefits.

ISBN: 9780170215718

A similar analysis is possible using the circular flow model for changes in imports.

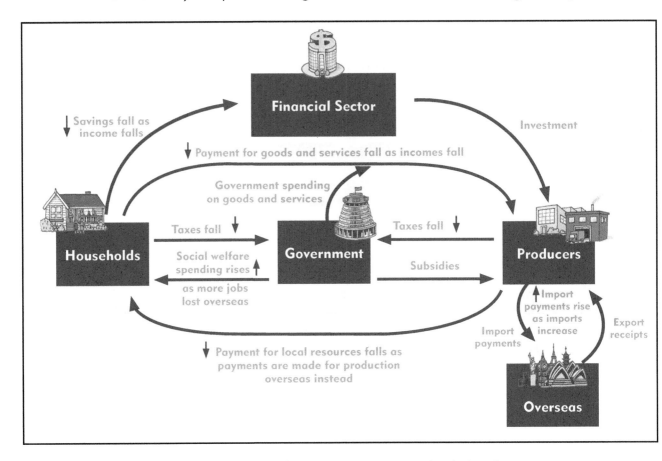

If imports rise (this is a withdrawal from the circular flow) then less income can be paid to households as payments are made overseas for goods and services. This is exacerbated if the imported goods replace New Zealand production directly.

- More jobs will be lost and/or wages will fall as payments are made to producers overseas (overseas workers).
- Households will experience falling incomes.
- Households will decrease their spending and/or savings as incomes rise.
- The government will receive less tax and increase spending on social welfare, e.g. unemployment benefits.
- There will be jobs created around the sale and distribution of imported goods. The production process (e.g. manufacturing) will decrease in the industries facing strong overseas competition. It is important to distinguish between subgroups of producers who may be benefitting from the trade and those that are hurt by the trade.

The circular flow model gives a good picture of all the groups affected by changes in trade.

ISBN: 9780170215718

1 Using your answers to question 1 page 100-101:
Analyse the effect of the change in productivity in Country B on various groups. In your answer you should **compare and contrast** the effect of the change in productivity on consumers and producers in Country A.

2 Using your answers to question 2 page 101:
Analyse the effect of the rising incomes in Country C on various groups. In your answer you should **compare and contrast** the effect of the change in incomes on the government and producers in Country C.

3 Using your analysis of question 3 page 101-102:
Analyse the effect of the change in productivity in New Zealand on various groups. In your answer you should **compare and contrast** the effect of a fall in domestic production of fish following the 2011 tsunami in Japan on consumers there and in New Zealand.

4 Using your analysis of question 4 page 102:
Analyse the effect of the change in productivity in New Zealand on various groups. In your answer you should **compare and contrast** the effect of growing consumer appreciation of the health benefits of organic production methods on importers and domestic producers in New Zealand.

5

Wood exports on growth spurt

Forestry and wood products put $4 billion into the economy and exports could soar during the next 20 years, according to NZ Wood.

A report by the Institute of Economic Research, commissioned by NZ Wood for the Wood Council of New Zealand, said that in the year to March the combined exports of forestry and wood-related products earned $4.6 billion, the sector making a direct contribution to gross domestic product of $4 billion.

a Illustrate, using the circular flow model, the effect of an increase in wood exports on the New Zealand economy.

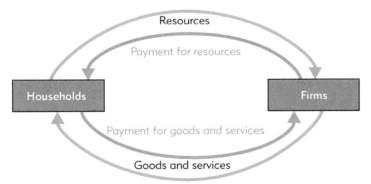

b Compare and contrast the effect of increased wood exports on New Zealand wood consumers and producers.

ISBN: 9780170215718

Economics for NCEA Level 2

3 ▪ Free Trade versus Protectionism

By the end of this unit you will be able to:

- Identify examples of protectionism.
- Distinguish between free trade and protectionism.
- Outline the arguments for and against free trade and protectionism.

Free trade is where the exchange of goods and services between countries is not restricted in any artificial way. **Protection** is an artificial barrier to free trade. While there has been a widespread move away from protection in recent years, there are still many forms of protection used. The most widely known are **tariffs**, **subsidies** and **quotas**. In addition to these there is the use of red tape or excessive **rules and regulations**. These are by no means the only forms of protection but they are the most basic.

Forms of protection

Import-restricting
A **tariff**: A tax on an imported commodity.
An **import quota**: A limit on the amount of a commodity that may enter a country.
Rules and regulations that create conditions under which goods can be imported excessively difficult.

Export-increasing
An **export subsidy**: Where the government pays exporters a sum of money for each unit of the product they export. This lowers the price of the exported good to make it more competitive overseas.

1 Classify each of the scenarios below as either **Tariff**, **Import Quota**, **Rules and Regulations** or **Export Subsidy**.
   a The EU allows fixed quantities of New Zealand butter into its markets.
   b Administrative obstacles impede access to markets.
   c New Zealand has a 19% tax on imports of clothing.
   d A payment from the government, making your product able to be sold at less than its costs of production, increasing its competitiveness internationally.
   e Australia banned New Zealand apples 1921–2010, on the grounds that they could spread the bacterial disease fireblight.
   f US sugar producers receive three times the world price for sugar through payments from their own government.
   g A tax put on imports making them more expensive and thus less competitive.
   h A limit to the number of goods entering a market.

2 Explain the difference between a tariff and an export subsidy.

3 Explain how tariffs, quotas and export subsidies affect production levels in an economy.

ISBN: 9780170215718

Arguments for and against free trade/protectionism

In theory, free trade is seen as benefiting the entire world. The arguments for it are:

- More efficient production results.
- Better use of resources worldwide.
- Consumers pay lower prices.
- Total world output will increase with greater specialisation.

In addition, free traders point out that the costs of supporting inefficient industries must be borne by someone — they argue there is no justification for one group to benefit at the expense of another.

While free trade has advantages for the whole world, there will be countries and industries that suffer in a shift from protection to free trade. Four commonly heard arguments for protection are:

- A new infant industry is given protection while it establishes itself. When it is able to compete, the protection can be removed.
- Because imports replace domestically produced goods, they also replace the producers of those goods, so imports will cause some loss of jobs in the domestic economy.
- Poor working conditions and low pay rates in some countries gives them an unfair advantage over countries like New Zealand, with its strict health and safety regulations and comparatively high wage rates.
- Political or strategic reasons. Some industries such as telecommunications are seen as essential. Agriculture has long been protected under this argument because in times of national emergency it is critical that a nation can feed itself.

The validity of these arguments, however, can be questioned:

- The infant industry argument accepts the value of free trade but asks only for short-term protection. The problem many industries have found is that by never experiencing competition they are never ready for it, and thus remain 'infants' all their lives.

Current New Zealand trade policy is one of free trade.

ISBN: 9780170215718

Economics for NCEA Level 2

- There will be a loss of jobs in some industries that face competition from cheaper imported goods. Unemployment should not be taken lightly as there are considerable social and economic costs associated with it. However, from an economic point of view, these workers were employed in an inefficient industry and over time they will move to efficient industries. The real problem is how much time this process takes.
- Low wage rates overseas may reflect low productivity, just as high wage rates here reflect high productivity.
- The essential industry argument is not economic in nature and so must be accepted or rejected on the strength of your belief in it. There are economic costs associated with protecting an inefficient industry but the non-economic risks of not having it may, in the population's mind, be fully justified.

Using the information in this unit, copy and complete these diagrams.

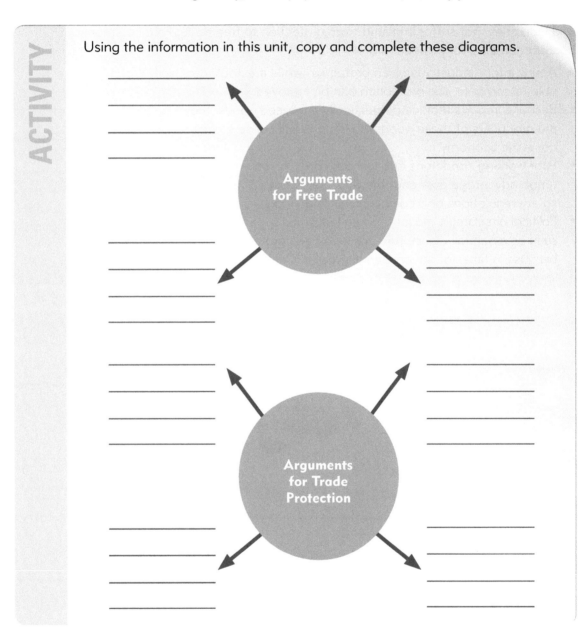

ISBN: 9780170215718

4 ▪ Exchange Rates

By the end of this unit you will be able to:

- Define an exchange rate.
- Calculate exchange rate transactions.
- Explain a floating exchange rate.
- Define an appreciation and a depreciation of a currency.

One of the major differences between regional and international trade is the added complication that there are different currencies used throughout the world. The **exchange rate** is the price of one currency expressed in terms of another. New Zealand has a floating exchange rate.

The exchange rate

Many of you have already encountered exchange rate systems. Perhaps you have travelled overseas and required different money, or overseas relatives may have sent you some money and this has needed to be changed into New Zealand's currency. **The exchange rate is the price of one currency expressed in terms of another.** For instance:

One New Zealand dollar (NZ$1) is worth	0.8061	dollar, Australia
	0.7733	dollar, United States
	0.7669	dollar, Canada
	0.3956	pound, United Kingdom
	0.4961	euro
	7191.70	rupiah, Indonesia
	5.8782	rand, South Africa
	33.016	rupee, India

ACTIVITY

1 Use the sample exchange rates provided above to calculate the value of the following currencies in New Zealand dollars.
- One Australian dollar
- One US dollar
- One Canadian dollar
- One British pound
- One euro
- One rupiah

2 Identify the country each currency name belongs to: *pounds, yen, won, rand, pula, real, rial, ringgit, pesos, kyat, renmindi, hryvnias, baht, dinars, kroner, rupee, bolivar, kwanza.*

ISBN: 9780170215718

Economics for NCEA Level 2

Where do these exchange rates come from?

There are many different methods used to determine the value of a particular currency. Prior to 1985 New Zealand operated a fixed exchange rate but since then the dollar has 'floated' (that is, the exchange rate was changed to a floating exchange rate regime).

Floating exchange rates

* Under a floating exchange rate, the market determines the price of the currency. The price of the currency is the equilibrium price.
* Under this exchange rate regime, an increase in the price is called an **appreciation** and a decrease in price is called a **depreciation**.

ACTIVITY

You have just returned from a round-the-world trip. You have carefully kept a record of all the spending you did in each country that you visited. You have written the information on a photograph taken in each country. The photographs and the amounts are shown below. Use the information to calculate the cost of your trip in current New Zealand dollars. You will need a copy of up-to-date exchange rates to complete this activity (or use the table on page 109).

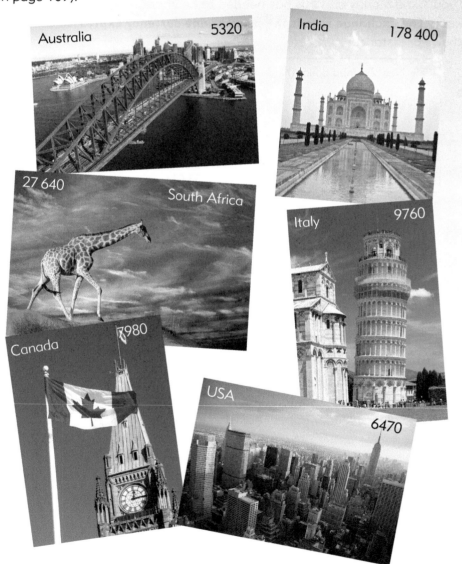

Australia 5320

India 178 400

27 640 South Africa

Italy 9760

Canada 7980

USA 6470

ISBN: 9780170215718

5 ▪ Effects of the Exchange Rate

By the end of this unit you will be able to:

- Use supply and demand to illustrate a floating exchange rate.
- Illustrate the depreciation and appreciation of the dollar using the supply and demand model.
- Outline the influences on the supply and demand for the New Zealand dollar.
- Explain how changes in the exchange rate can affect the quantities imported and exported.

Our understanding of the supply and demand model allows us to illustrate how **the exchange rate is determined under a floating exchange rate regime**. The changes in the price of the currency are easily seen using graphical analysis. The usefulness of an overall exchange rate figure is explored and the Trade Weighted Index (TWI) introduced. The impact of exchange rates on import and export levels is the final influence explained.

Floating exchange rates and the supply and demand model

New Zealand dollars can generally only be spent in New Zealand. Anyone wanting to buy anything in New Zealand must use New Zealand dollars. This means that overseas individuals or firms must buy New Zealand dollars before they can buy anything here. This creates a **demand for New Zealand dollars**. The demand for New Zealand dollars is determined by:

- Exports (selling goods and services overseas) including tourists coming here.
- Overseas investment here (determined by interest rates).
- Borrowing from abroad.
- Return of investment income to New Zealand.

Likewise, New Zealanders who want to buy anything overseas must sell their New Zealand dollars in order to buy overseas currency. This creates the **supply of New Zealand dollars**. The supply of New Zealand dollars is determined by:

- Imports (buying goods and services overseas) including New Zealand tourists travelling overseas.
- New Zealand investment overseas.
- Repayment of loans.
- Investment income sent to overseas investors.

Factors of supply and demand are shown in the graph at the top of the next page.

ISBN: 9780170215718

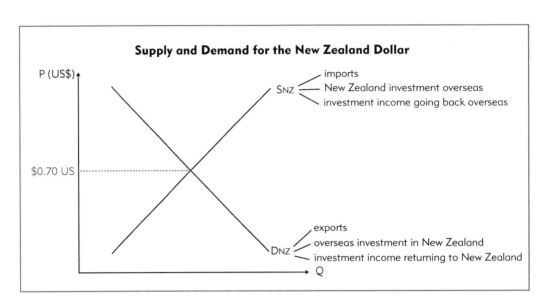

Supply and Demand for the New Zealand Dollar

Illustrating an appreciation or depreciation of the New Zealand dollar

If the levels of demand or supply of the New Zealand dollar change, a shift of the relevant curve and a change in the price of the New Zealand dollar will occur.

EXAMPLE 1

An increase in the numbers of tourists coming to New Zealand to see our geothermal wonderland:
⇒ results in a greater demand for the New Zealand dollar
⇒ shifts the demand curve right
⇒ causes the price of the New Zealand dollar to increase.

The New Zealand dollar will appreciate.

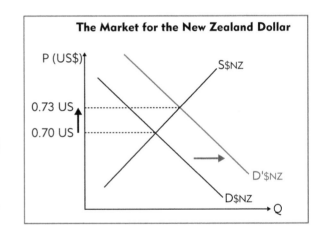

EXAMPLE 2

The price of oil rises, increasing value of imports. This will:
⇒ result in a greater supply of the New Zealand dollar as oil importers sell NZ$ to buy US$ to buy oil
⇒ shift the supply curve right
⇒ cause the price of the New Zealand dollar to decrease.

The New Zealand dollar will depreciate.

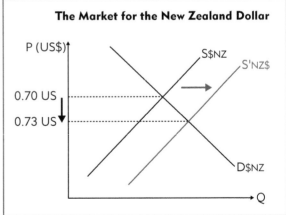

ISBN: 9780170215718

1 Draw a fully labelled 'Market for the New Zealand dollar'.
   a Show how New Zealanders buying more Italian made goods following an Italian Film Festival would affect the value of the New Zealand dollar.
   b Explain the changes you made to your graph in **a**.

2 Draw a fully labelled 'Market for the New Zealand dollar'.
   a Show how terrorist attacks in India reducing New Zealand tourist numbers to India would affect the value of the New Zealand dollar.
   b Explain the changes you made to your graph in **a**.

3 Draw a fully labelled 'Market for the New Zealand dollar'.
   a Show how widespread tension in the Middle East and a consequent rise in the price of oil would affect the value of the New Zealand dollar.
   b Explain the changes you made to your graph in **a**.

4 Draw a fully labelled 'Market for the New Zealand dollar'.
   a Show how a rise in New Zealand interest rates would affect the value of the New Zealand dollar.
   b Explain the changes you made to your graph in **a**.

The Trade Weighted Index

Each currency of the world has an individual exchange rate against the New Zealand dollar. Getting an overall picture of the state of the New Zealand dollar is difficult since it is rising and falling against different currencies at different times. The Trade Weighted Index (TWI) is a summary statistic of the strength of the New Zealand dollar. It is based on the exchange rates of five currencies: United States dollar, United Kingdom pound, euro (which replaced the German mark in 1999), Japanese yen, and the Australian dollar.

> The TWI (Trade Weighted Index) is a weighted average of a basket of other currencies.

As its name suggests, these currencies are **weighted**. (Compare this to the CPI, another weighted index, on page 23.) The currencies are weighted according to the relative share of merchandise trade (both imports and exports). They are also weighted against the relative size of each country's GDP.

The Reserve Bank of New Zealand calculates the TWI. The current weightings were introduced in 1999 following an extensive review, and are adjusted annually.

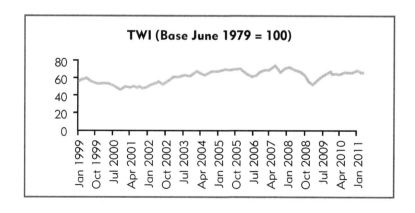

ISBN: 9780170215718

1 Explain what a rise in the TWI means in terms of the value of the New Zealand dollar.
   a Explain how this affects import prices in New Zealand.
   b Explain how this affects New Zealand's export competitiveness.

2 Explain what a fall in the TWI means in terms of the value of the New Zealand dollar.
   a Explain how this affects import prices in New Zealand.
   b Explain how this affects New Zealand's export competitiveness.

3 With reference to the TWI data on page 113, explain the effect that changes in the TWI between November 2008 and August 2009 had on:
   a New Zealand firms importing raw materials.
   b New Zealand exporters.

4 With reference to the TWI data on page 113, explain the effect that changes in the TWI between December 2007 and November 2008 had on:
   a New Zealand firms importing raw materials.
   b New Zealand exporters.

The effect of exchange rate changes on the level of imports or exports

Exports

New Zealand is generally a price-taker in the markets to which it exports. The world market determines the world price and as a small participant we are unable to influence this price. Also, world prices are generally expressed in US dollars. If the price is given in US dollars, then the actual amount received by New Zealand exporters is determined by the current exchange rate. For example, if the world price of lamb is US$10 per lamb, the money received in New Zealand dollars will depend upon the exchange rate.

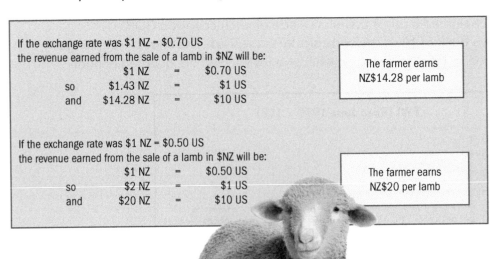

If the exchange rate was $1 NZ = $0.70 US the revenue earned from the sale of a lamb in $NZ will be:

	$1 NZ	=	$0.70 US
so	$1.43 NZ	=	$1 US
and	$14.28 NZ	=	$10 US

The farmer earns NZ$14.28 per lamb

If the exchange rate was $1 NZ = $0.50 US the revenue earned from the sale of a lamb in $NZ will be:

	$1 NZ	=	$0.50 US
so	$2 NZ	=	$1 US
and	$20 NZ	=	$10 US

The farmer earns NZ$20 per lamb

If the NZ dollar appreciates, it makes NZ exports **less competitive** internationally; **exports fall** as less is sold overseas.

If the NZ dollar depreciates, it makes NZ exports **more competitive** internationally; **exports rise** as more is sold overseas.

Imports

A similar analysis for imports applies.

If the world price of oil is US$100 a barrel, the price of oil in NZ$ will depend upon the exchange rate.

If the exchange rate was $1 NZ = $0.70 US
the cost of a US$100 barrel of oil in New Zealand will be:

	$1 NZ	=	$0.70 US
so	$1.43 NZ	=	$1 US
and	$142.86 NZ	=	$100 US

The barrel will cost
$NZ142.86

If the exchange rate was $1 NZ = $0.50 US
the cost of a US$100 barrel of oil in New Zealand will be:

	$1 NZ	=	$0.50 US
so	$2 NZ	=	$1 US
and	$200 NZ	=	$100 US

The barrel will cost
$NZ200

ACTIVITY

1 Stainless steel bolts imported into New Zealand are priced at US$10 a carton.

   a Calculate the cost of the carton if the exchange rate is NZ$1 = US$ 0.45.

   b Calculate the cost of the carton if the exchange rate is NZ$1 = US$ 0.65.

   c Has the New Zealand exchange rate appreciated or depreciated between **a** and **b**?

   d Calculate the cost of the carton if the exchange rate is NZ$1 = US$ 0.25.

   e Has the New Zealand exchange rate appreciated or depreciated between **a** and **d**?

   f Explain the effect of:

   i An appreciation on the cost of imports priced in terms of the other currency.

   ii A depreciation on the cost of imports priced in terms of the other currency.

2 Wood pulp exported from New Zealand is priced at US$50 a tonne.

   a Calculate the cost of a tonne if the exchange rate is NZ$1 = US$ 0.30.

Economics for NCEA Level 2

ACTIVITY

b Calculate the cost of a tonne if the exchange rate is NZ$1 = US$ 0.75.

c Has the New Zealand exchange rate appreciated or depreciated between **a** and **b**?

d Calculate the cost of a tonne if the exchange rate is NZ$1 = US$ 0.15.

e Has the New Zealand exchange rate appreciated or depreciated between **a** and **d**?

f Explain the effect of:

   i An appreciation of the $NZ on the return on exports priced in terms of the other currency.

   ii A depreciation of the $NZ on the return on exports priced in terms of the other currency.

3 New Zealand is generally a price-taker on international markets. Explain the importance of our exchange rate to:

a Our export earnings.

b Our cost of imports.

4 Explain the effect of the change in the value of the New Zealand dollar on each of the firms described below. The first one is done for you as an example.

Example: A small manufacturing firm in Blenheim, which imports resins from India to make a product sold in New Zealand, is affected by a falling NZ$.

Explanation: Depreciation of the NZ$ causes the cost of imported raw materials to rise, profit margins are squeezed or the firm must put up prices, possibly causing sales/revenue to fall, possibly causing job losses long term.

a	An exporter of New Zealand-made goods affected by a rising NZ$.
b	The weakening NZ$ has affected the US movie making industry's decisions regarding New Zealand as a location to shoot its films.
c	A manufacturing firm in Napier, which imports specialty goods from the Middle East, is affected by a falling NZ$.
d	Tourist operators are concerned by rises in the NZ$.
e	An importer of Canadian-made jewellery is affected by the rising NZ$.
f	Farmers in Canterbury are affected by the rising NZ$.
g	Electronics and whiteware from Asia imported into New Zealand is affected by a falling NZ$.
h	New Zealand-produced wines sold into the US are affected by a falling NZ$.
i	Fresh fruit imported from Samoa is affected by a rising NZ$.

5 a Identify which groups in New Zealand benefit from an appreciation of the New Zealand dollar.

b Identify which groups in New Zealand benefit from a depreciation in the New Zealand dollar.

c Explain whether or not the needs of both groups can be met at the same time.

ISBN: 9780170215718

6 ▪ The Balance of Payments and International Investment Position

By the end of this unit you will be able to:

- Identify the major components of the Balance of Payments.
- Classify transactions within the Balance of Payments.
- Analyse the changes over time in New Zealand's Balance of Payments.
- Explain the Terms of Trade statistic.
- Explain the link between Terms of Trade and Balance of Payments.

Statistics New Zealand regularly surveys businesses to **measure the size and composition of the goods and services** traded between New Zealand and the rest of the world. These statistics are used to compile **the New Zealand Balance of Payments (BOP) and International Investment Position (IIP)**.

The Balance of Payments and International Investment Position: The major components

The **Balance of Payments and International Investment Position** records New Zealand's transactions with the rest of the world. Essentially it measures all flows of money in and out of New Zealand. It gives a good picture of the value of New Zealand's trade.

The Balance of Payments is made up of three sections. These sections are called **accounts**. The three accounts are:

1 The **Current Account**, which measures all:
- Exports and imports of goods — **Balance on Goods**
- Exports and imports of services — **Balance on Services**
- Investment income earned and paid — **Balance on Income**
- Resources supplied to, or received from, overseas without payment required — **Balance on Current Transfers**.

2 The **Capital Account,** which measures all capital transfers and the purchase or sale of non-produced, non-financial assets. These transactions relate generally to assets becoming New Zealand owned because of a change in the residency or citizenship of the owner. That is, they relate largely to immigrants transferring their assets here. Previously these types of transactions were recorded under Transfers.

3 The **Financial Account**, which measures all transactions involving New Zealand's purchases of assets overseas or increases in liabilities to overseas residents.

The Current Account and the Capital Account record New Zealand's transactions in goods, services, income and transfers with non-residents. The Financial Account records financial transactions involving New Zealand claims on assets and liabilities to non-residents.

The Financial Account shows the flows in and out of balances (or stocks) of assets and liabilities recorded in the International Investment Position.

ISBN: 9780170215718

The International Investment Position (IIP) records the balances of the assets and liabilities held by New Zealanders overseas and the assets and liabilities held in New Zealand by overseas residents at a particular point in time. The types of items recorded in each account are shown in more detail below.

THE CURRENT ACCOUNT

i)   Export of Goods

Less   Import of Goods

Equals   The Balance on Goods

ii)   Export of Services

Less   Import of Services

Equals   Balance on Services

iii)   Plus   Balance on Current Transfers

iv)   Plus   Balance on Income

Equals   **Balance on the Current Account**

Explanatory Notes
- The receipts from the sales of goods overseas minus the payments for goods bought overseas gives us the **Balance on Goods**.
- Similarly, the receipts from the sales of **services** overseas minus the payments for **services** purchased overseas gives us the **Balance on Services**.
- **Transfers** are one-way transactions that do not require a corresponding payment in return. Examples include foreign aid, benefits paid to other governments in respect of New Zealanders living abroad (and vice versa) and non-resident withholding tax.
- **Balance on Income** is income for New Zealand investors from their investments overseas, and the income for overseas investors from their investments in New Zealand.
- Finally the **Balance on Goods** is added to the **Balance on Services**, **Balance on Current Transfers** and **Balance on Income** to give the **Balance on the Current Account**.

THE CAPITAL ACCOUNT

          Capital Inflows

Less   Capital Outflows

Equals   **Balance on Capital Account**

Explanatory Notes
The inflows and outflows are made up of the following two components:
- **Capital Transfers** involve the transfer of ownership of fixed assets or the transfer of funds linked to them without any counterpart transaction, e.g. new immigrants transferring their wealth to New Zealand.
- **Non-produced Non-financial Assets** include such things as patents and copyrights. They are intangible assets.

THE FINANCIAL ACCOUNT

          Portfolio Investment

Plus   Direct Investment

Plus   Other Capital

Plus   Reserve Assets

Plus   Net Errors and Omissions

Equals   **Balance on Financial Account**

Explanatory Notes
These figures are all net (inflow minus outflow):
- **Portfolio Investment** involves the buying of less than 10% of an asset. The funds are generally in the form of managed funds.
- **Direct Investment** involves the buying of more than 10% of an asset.
- **Other Capital** is other capital investment.
- **Net Errors and Omissions** is a rounding figure to ensure that the Balance of Payments always balances, that is, adds to zero.
- **Reserve Assets** are RBNZ and Treasury funds.

ISBN: 9780170215718

- The asset and liabilities transactions recorded in the Financial Account give rise to the international investment income recorded in the Current Account, e.g. interest or dividends earned on investment.
- As the Balance of Payments adds to zero, the information called the Balance of Payments by newspapers and television is generally just the Balance on Current Account.

CURRENT ACCOUNT + CAPITAL ACCOUNT + FINANCIAL ACCOUNT = BALANCE OF PAYMENTS

ACTIVITY

1 Using the words provided below, copy and complete the Balance of Payments structured overview that follows.

Balance of Payments	Import of Goods	Import of Services
Portfolio Investment	Capital Outflows	Capital Inflows
Financial Account	Capital Account	Other Capital
Export of Goods	Balance on Current Transfers
Balance on Income	Current Account	Direct Investment
Balance on Services	Net Errors and Omissions
Export of Services	Balance on Goods	Reserve Assets

Balance of Payments: Structured Overview

ISBN: 9780170215718

2   For each of the scenarios given below identify which category within
    the Balance of Payments the transaction would affect.

| Categories | | | | | | | |
Exports of Goods	Imports of Goods	Exports of Services	Imports of Services	Balance on Current Transfers	Balance on Income	Balance on Capital Account	Balance on Financial Account

a	New Zealand imports of used cars from Japan fall.
b	New Zealand insurance firm insures property in Australia.
c	Rent received from tenants in a building in Hong Kong owned by a New Zealand firm.
d	Loan given to New Zealand firm by a Japanese bank.
e	Interest paid by a New Zealand firm to a German finance company.
f	Carpets made in New Zealand sold to Canada.
g	Steel produced in Eastern Europe bought by a New Zealand company.
h	Steel manufactured in Wiri sold to Taiwan.
i	Venture finance capital lent to a company in Samoa.
j	Telecom dividend paid to shareholders in Australia.
k	New Zealand beer exported to Australia.
l	Insurance companies buy reinsurance from British underwriters.
m	Record numbers of tourists visit New Zealand during the Rugby World Cup 2011.

3   For each of the scenarios given below identify which category within
    the Balance of Payments the transaction would affect. Use the
    categories provided in the previous question.

a	New Zealanders travel on United Emirates airline to Dubai.
b	Greater sales of New Zealand butter to the EU following changes in quota agreements.
c	Ukrainian computer software consultants do contract work for New Zealand firms.
d	Indian film companies use editing suites in New Zealand.
e	Fonterra receives profits from their Australian companies.
f	New Zealand sends financial contribution to the UN.
g	Hong Kong finance companies purchase a building in Wellington CBD.
h	Increased fish exports to Korea.
i	New car imports from the UK increase.
j	Increased sales of cheese to South America.
k	New Zealanders travel to the Gold Coast on Qantas.
l	American movie companies film in the South Island.
m	New Zealand animal medicines exported worldwide.

ISBN-9780170215718

4 a Explain how the Balance on Trade is calculated.
  b Explain how the Balance on Services is calculated.
  c Explain how the Balance on the Current Account is calculated.

5 Identify where the following transactions would be recorded within the Balance of Payments. Be as accurate as you can.
  a A recent immigrant to New Zealand becomes a permanent resident and transfers their assets to New Zealand.
  b A British tourist buys a ticket on Air New Zealand.
  c Australian shipping firms use New Zealand port facilities.
  d New Zealand farmers earn record prices on the sale of butter.
  e Imports of cars from Korea increase.
  f Swedish company buys New Zealand pulp and paper mill.
  g Dairy commodity prices push up the value of exports.
  h Imports from China fall.
  i New Zealand dairy giant Fonterra buys a milk processing plant in Wales.
  j Exports to Australia rise.
  k Increasing numbers of New Zealand families take up Australian citizenship and transfer assets there.
  l New Zealanders fly on Qantas to Honolulu.

6 Explain what the International Investment Position (IIP) shows.

7 Explain the difference between the Financial Account of the Balance of Payments and the IIP.

8 Explain how a change in the Balance on Income is linked to the Financial Account.

9 Explain how the Balance on Income and the Financial Account are related.

10 Use the information provided in the following table to calculate the balances below.

Balance of Payments Major Components	2010 NZ$ (million)
Exports of goods	40 092
Exports of services	12 332
Income from investment abroad	4495
Inflow of current transfers	2003
Imports of goods	37 451
Imports of services	12 239
Income from foreign investment in New Zealand	12 268
Outflow of current transfers	1422
Capital account inflow	1064
Capital account outflow	1401
New Zealand investment abroad	11 758
Foreign investment in New Zealand	13 138

a Balance on Goods
b Balance on Services
c Balance on Income
d Balance on Current Transfers
e Balance on Current Account
f Balance on Capital Account
g Balance on Financial Account
h Net Errors and Omissions

ISBN: 9780170215718

11 Use the information provided in the following table to calculate the balances below.

Balance of Payments Major Components	2008 NZ$ (million)	2009 NZ$ (million)
Exports of goods	38 717	44 247
Capital account outflow	1677	1401
Outflow of current transfers	1396	1483
Imports of services	12 631	13 827
Income from foreign investment in New Zealand	19 917	18 052
Inflow of current transfers	2094	2337
Capital account inflow	1677	1635
Exports of services	12 890	12 949
New Zealand investment abroad	13 237	
Direct investment		-1027
Portfolio investment		-1564
Other investment		-4008
Reserve assets		-9999
Foreign investment in New Zealand	26 416	
Direct investment		4640
Portfolio investment		-18 729
Other investment		-904
Income from investment abroad	6373	4876
Imports of goods	40 515	45 770

a Balance on Goods
  i 2008   **ii** 2009

b Balance on Services
  i 2008   **ii** 2009

c Balance on Income
  i 2008   **ii** 2009

d Balance on Current Transfers
  i 2008   **ii** 2009

e Balance on Current Account
  i 2008   **ii** 2009

f Balance on Capital Account
  i 2008   **ii** 2009

g Balance on Financial Account
  i 2008   **ii** 2009

h Net Errors and Omissions
  i 2008   **ii** 2009

i Explain what the Balance of Payments show.

j Explain what net errors and omissions represent.

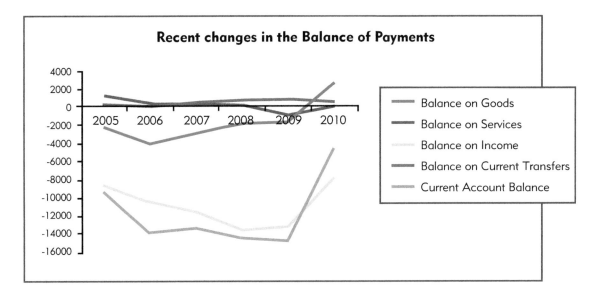

Recent changes in the Balance of Payments

Legend:
- Balance on Goods
- Balance on Services
- Balance on Income
- Balance on Current Transfers
- Current Account Balance

Overseas Terms of Trade index

The overseas Terms of Trade index measures the changing volume of imports that can be funded by a unit volume of New Zealand's exports, in other words the quantity of imports that can be bought with a given unit of exports (e.g. how many litres of oil can be bought with one tonne of butter). The index is calculated as the ratio of the total export price index to the total import price index.

$$\text{Terms of Trade} = \frac{P_X}{P_M} \times 1000 \quad \text{where}$$

both P_X and P_M are index numbers

P_X: price of exports
P_M: price of imports

An increase in the Terms of Trade index indicates that the real purchasing power of exports has increased, while a decrease indicates a drop in the purchasing power of exports. An index value above 1000 indicates the Terms of Trade are more *favourable* than the average for the 1980–89 base period. An index value below 1000 indicates the Terms of Trade are *less favourable* than the average for the 1980–89 period.

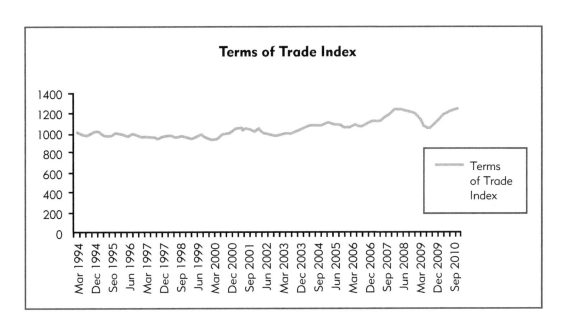

Terms of Trade Index

Legend:
- Terms of Trade Index

ISBN: 9780170215718

ISBN: 9780170215718

ACTIVITY

1 Describe what Terms of Trade means.

2 Explain the meaning of a favourable movement in the Terms of Trade.

3 Explain the meaning of an unfavourable movement in the Terms of Trade.

4 Explain the impact of a favourable movement in the Terms of Trade on the Balance of Trade.

5 Explain the difference between:
   a The Terms of Trade and the TWI.
   b The Terms of Trade and Balance of Trade.
   c The TWI and the Balance of Trade.

6 Copy and complete the following table for the country of Yendor.

Year	Export Price Index	Import Price Index	Terms of Trade	Favourable or unfavourable	Explanation
1999	1000	1200	833	–	Requires previous year's data to assess
2000	1133	1221	928	Favourable	Export prices rose by more than import prices rose
2001	1140	1180			
2002	1145	1300			
2003	1130	1150			
2004	1125	1148			
2005	1010	1050			
2006	990	998			

The link between the Terms of Trade and the Balance of Payments

The Terms of Trade reflect the relative prices of exports and imports. There is no measure of the quantities traded. (This is different from the Balance of Payments, which reflects the value, i.e. price and quantity, of the goods traded.)

If the volume of trade is relatively stable then a favourable movement in our Terms of Trade will result in a positive movement in the Balance on Goods.

ACTIVITY

1 Explain why a drop in the Terms of Trade index is a worry to New Zealand.

2 Outline the level of control New Zealand has over its Terms of Trade.

3 Outline how being a major agricultural exporter affects New Zealand's Terms of Trade.

4 Explain how the types of goods we import affect our Terms of Trade.

5 Outline how New Zealand might improve its Terms of Trade.

7 ▪ The Impacts of Trade

By the end of this unit you will be able to:

- Measure the importance of trade to the New Zealand economy.
- Analyse the impacts of changes in international trade on various groups in New Zealand society.

The importance of trade

The first units of the trade topic outlined the reasons for and the benefits of trade. These reasons are particularly relevant for small economies. New Zealand produces a narrow range of goods from a narrow range of resources. Given the range and quality of goods that New Zealanders require, we must import. Our domestic market is small and can generate only a small amount of income for New Zealanders. If we are to enjoy higher standards of living and growth, we must trade.

A common statistic used to indicate the importance of trade is **exports as a percentage of GDP**. Another statistic is **Current Account as a percentage of GDP**.

Exports as a percentage of GDP

This shows how much of all production is sold overseas. As GDP is a measure of national income, this measure shows the proportion of our national income generated by exports.

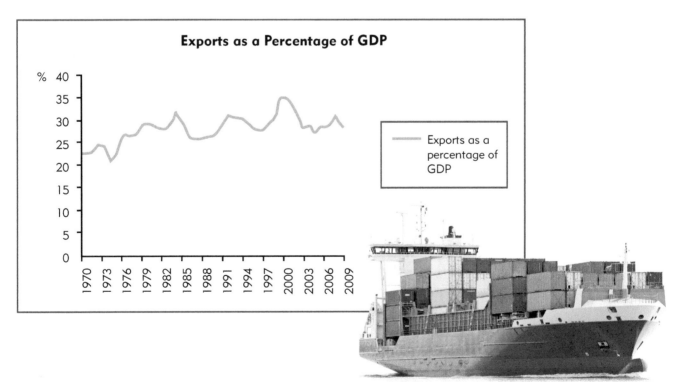

ISBN: 9780170215718

Economics for NCEA Level 2

Current Account as a percentage of GDP

This shows the amount of GDP over and above exports required to pay for our imports. One accepted standard of the sustainability of a Current Account deficit is its value relative to the country's total level of production, measured as Gross Domestic Product (GDP). The graph below suggests that since 1995 the deficit has fairly often been more than 6% of GDP, and especially so since 2005. Some critics have suggested that 6% is at the top range of a sustainable Current-Account-to-GDP ratio.

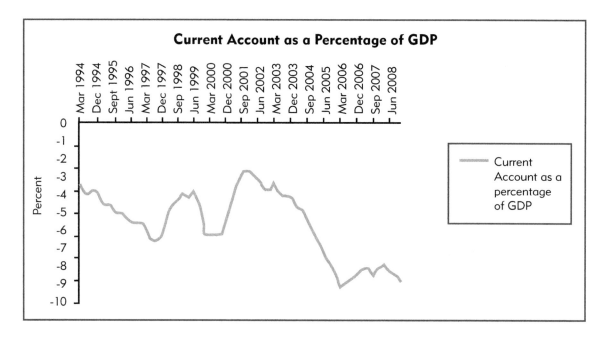

Current Account as a Percentage of GDP

ACTIVITY

1 Based on the exports as a percentage of the GDP statistic, comment on the importance of trade to New Zealand.

2 Based on the Current Account as a percentage of the GDP statistic, comment on the importance of trade to New Zealand.

The links between changes in trade and various groups in New Zealand society

The circular flow model can be used to show how increased exports feed through the economy affecting different groups. Obviously, a fall in exports will have the opposite effect.

While this gives an overall view, the benefits will go to the geographical regions of New Zealand affected directly by the increased trade. The rural sector will be the first to benefit from higher agricultural commodity prices. Initially the increased employment will be industry specific but as these employed workers spend, the benefits start to be spread wider. Towns servicing the rural communities will enjoy the early benefits of increased spending.

Consequently, a downturn in exports can be felt more sharply and for a longer period in a local or regional economy, before the wider impacts are felt by the rest of the country.

ISBN: 9780170215718

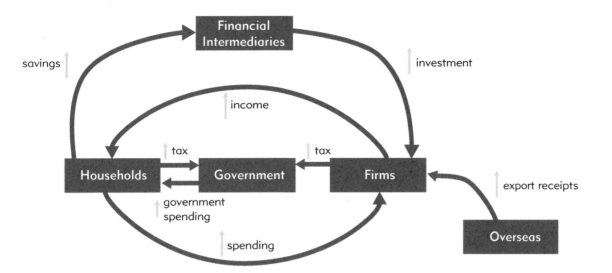

ISBN: 9780170215718

ACTIVITY

1 The 2011 Rugby World Cup semi-finals and final were played at Eden Park in Auckland. Explain how this impacted on:
   a Local businesses, in and around the central Auckland area.
   b Tourist operators in Rotorua and Queenstown.
   c Firms, based throughout New Zealand, which provide goods and services to these businesses.

Read the article on the next page and answer the following:

2 Outline what Fonterra is.

3 Describe the why Fonterra payout to farmers is high.

4 Define the term commodity prices.

5 Use the circular flow model to explain the ripple effect this will have on the wider New Zealand economy.

6 Explain how the increase in sales by Fonterra to China will affect:
   a The value of the New Zealand dollar. Use the supply and demand model to support your answer.
   b The $NZ and how this will affect New Zealand importers and consumers.

Economics for NCEA Level 2

Fonterra unveils record payout

By Owen Hembry

NZ Herald **Tuesday May 24, 2011**

Fonterra is forecasting another record payout, but warns that prices could slip back again next year.

Fonterra has pushed its forecast payout to another record high — but global supply, commodity prices and currency value could see it slip back next season, says the dairy giant.

The farmer co-operative yesterday increased by 10c its forecast payout before retentions for the 2010/11 season to $8-$8.10 — combining a milk price of $7.50 a kilogram of milksolids and a distributable profit of 50c-60c a share.

Fonterra last week said it was on track for record production, more than 4 per cent ahead of the same time last year, with the season finishing at the end of this month. The final payout will be confirmed in September.

An $8.10 payout based on a 4 per cent rise in production could be worth about $10.8 billion — with each percentage point rise adding more than $100 million.

However, the opening forecast for the 2011/12 season was a lower $7.15-$7.25 before retentions, including a milk price of $6.75 a kilogram of milk solids and a distributable profit range of 40c-50c a share.

Chairman Sir Henry van der Heyden said the opening forecast for the coming season reflected a realistic outlook towards global dairy markets.

"In the current season, farmers have benefited from sharply higher commodity prices due to improved world demand for dairy products."

Although market prices and exchange rates would yield a milk price similar to the current season, commodity prices had started to drift down while the New Zealand dollar remained high, van der Heyden said.

"As commodities are mostly sold in US dollars, a higher exchange rate hits the milk price."

Fonterra collected about 89 per cent of national milk production in 2009–10.

Chief executive Andrew Ferrier said he was pleased to see international prices stabilise, although current prices were well down on the highs of a few months ago.

"But I think this issue of volatility is still absolutely here to stay."

Operating earnings within the commodities and ingredients businesses and the consumer-brands businesses in total were expected to be marginally ahead of 2010 in spite of the strong global commodity prices.

A payout for the new season before retentions of $7.15-$7.25 would be a good return for farmers, Ferrier said. "It would still be the third-best payout, I think, in the history of the industry."

Shareholders' Council chairman Simon Couper said there could be no doubt dairying was the engine powering the economy.

"We have hit the trifecta for the country — record payout and production for this season and a record opening forecast for next season."

Federated Farmers Dairy chairman Lachlan McKenzie said farmers would be happy with the opening forecast for the new season.

"We're saying 'be aware of that volatility, be conservative'. Farmers that have to will be paying off debt, ensure that we focus on the fundamentals that are going to increase profitability, not just increase your costs."

BNZ chief economist Doug Steel said the new season payout would generate strong on-farm profitability and was positive for the economy.

Steel has forecast industry production to rise by 4-5 per cent in the coming season, reflecting some of the underlying growth from land being converted to dairying.

Strong demand from emerging markets, including China, was supporting international dairy markets, Steel said.

"China's market share of New Zealand dairy products has increased to around 20 per cent by value over the past year, from around 5 per cent only three years ago," he said.

"This is part of the wider Asian growth story, which New Zealand dairy and wider New Zealand agriculture is well placed to tap into."

A 4.5 per cent rise in production for Fonterra next year, on top of a 4 per cent rise this season with a $7.25 payout, could equate to a potential payout of about $10.1 billion.

ISBN: 9780170215718

8 ▪ Government Policies and Trade

> **By the end of this unit you will be able to:**
>
> - Understand how government policy measures can be designed to influence trade.
> - Explain how government policies can be designed to promote or restrict trade (including exchange rate policy and trade agreements).

The New Zealand government is committed to a policy of free trade. Protection for New Zealand producers has been gradually phased out, as have export subsidies. These actions have been largely unilateral. This means our trading partners did not also remove protections as part of an agreement to free up trade. The nature of our exports (agricultural) means we are trading in one of the most highly protected areas of world trade. In addition the other agricultural export nations tend to be economically weak. There are other policies open to the government that they do not use. These include exchange rate policies and monetary policies.

Exchange rate policies

As outlined previously, New Zealand has a floating exchange rate. It is a 'clean float', meaning the government does not actively intervene in the foreign exchange market, buying and selling currencies to manipulate the price of the New Zealand dollar (i.e. the exchange rate).

While current monetary policy primarily targets price stability, it should be noted that by manipulating interest rates to influence prices, exchange rates may also be affected.

For example, when interest rates are increased, this tends to encourage net foreign investment in New Zealand, leading to an appreciation of the NZ$ through an increase in demand. However, the primary focus of monetary policy does not relate to exchange rate.

Promotion of trade

The New Zealand government promotes exports through New Zealand Trade and Enterprise. This organisation was formed in July 2003 when Trade New Zealand and Industry New Zealand merged.

New Zealand Trade and Enterprise aims to improve the capability and international competitiveness of New Zealand businesses. They are able to provide market intelligence and market development services through their network of offices in New Zealand and around the world.

Trade agreements

The New Zealand government actively pursues free trade within the World Trade Organisation (WTO) and by trying to negotiate trade agreements with other specific countries.

ISBN: 9780170215718

CER is a series of agreements and arrangements that began with the Australia New Zealand Closer Economic Trade Relations Agreement (ANZCERTA) on 1 January 1983. CER is one of the most comprehensive, effective and mutually beneficial free trade agreements in the world.

There are two major types of trade agreement:

Customs unions: Where the member nations have a free trade agreement between themselves, and a common external trade policy for non-members. An example is the European Union (EU). The EU is also an example of a multilateral trade agreement, involving three or more partners.

Free trade areas: Where the member nations have free trade between themselves but their own independent external trade policy for non-members. An example is Closer Economic Relations (CER) between New Zealand and Australia. CER is also an example of a bilateral trade agreement, involving two partners only.

THE WTO

This organisation grew out of the now defunct General Agreement on Tariffs and Trade (GATT). The WTO is a rules-based, member-driven organisation — all decisions are made by the member governments, and the rules are the outcome of negotiations among members.

FACT FILE

Location: Geneva, Switzerland
Established: 1 January 1995
Created by: Uruguay round negotiations (1986–94)
Membership: 153 countries (as of 2008)
Budget: 185 million Swiss francs for 2008
Secretariat staff: 635
Head: Pascal Lamy (Director-General)
Functions:
- Administering WTO trade agreements
- Forum for trade negotiations
- Handling trade disputes
- Monitoring national trade policies
- Technical assistance and training for developing countries
- Cooperation with other international organisations

The current round of negotiations is the Doha round. Doha was the location of the initial talks in 2001. The last round was the 1987 Uruguay round, where agriculture was first put on the agenda.
Website: www.wto.org

World trade and production have accelerated
Both trade and GDP fell in the late 1920s, before bottoming out in 1932. After the Second World War, both have risen exponentially, most of the time with trade outpacing GDP.

(1950 = 100. Trade and GDP: log scale.)

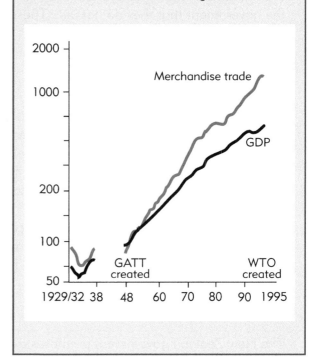

APEC and the Cairns Group

New Zealand is also a member of APEC (Asia-Pacific Economic Cooperation). Formed in 1989, APEC member economies work together to sustain this economic growth through a commitment to open trade, investment and economic reform.

The Cairns Group is a coalition of 19 agricultural exporting countries, which account for over 25 percent of the world's agricultural exports. Members of the group are: Argentina, Australia, Bolivia, Brazil, Canada, Chile, Colombia, Costa Rica, Guatemala, Indonesia, Malaysia, New Zealand, Pakistan, Paraguay, Peru, Philippines, South Africa, Thailand and Uruguay.

ISBN: 9780170215718

Free Trade Agreements

The Ministry provides policy and negotiating advice in the areas of trade rules, technical barriers to trade, competition, intellectual property and government procurement. The Ministry also plays a central role in the market access / tariff negotiations.

Regional and bilateral free trade agreements have become an important part of New Zealand's international trade policy. New Zealand has used free trade agreements / closer economic partnerships to liberalise trade between economies. A Closer Economic Partnership Agreement with Thailand was negotiated in 2004 and implemented in 2005. Negotiations

for a Free Trade Agreement with Chile, Brunei and Singapore known as the Trans Pacific Strategic Economic Partnership were concluded in 2005. Negotiations for further agreements with Malaysia, China and the Association of South East Asian countries are underway.

The Ministry gives particularly high priority to the negotiation of a free trade agreement with China. We support the trade negotiating effort through our participation in domestic consultations and the development of a parallel work programme with a key Chinese regulatory authority.

Source: Ministry of Economic Development

ACTIVITY

1 Outline New Zealand's international trade policy.

2 Identify the trade organisations New Zealand is a member of.

3 Identify what ANZCER stands for.

4 Explain the term free trade.

5 Outline the advantages of free trade.

6 Outline the disadvantages of free trade.

7 Explain what is meant by protectionism.

8 Outline the advantages of protectionism.

9 Outline the disadvantages of protectionism.

Read the article on the next page and answer the following:

10 Explain the role played by WTO in the apple dispute.

11 Explain how Australia uses protection to keep New Zealand apples out.

12 Use the supply and demand model to show the effect of New Zealand apples gaining access to the Australian market.

13 Compare and contrast the effect the new access will have on:
a Australian apple growers.
b New Zealand apple growers.

14 Compare and contrast the effect the new access will have on:
a Australian apple consumers.
b New Zealand apple consumers.

15 New Zealand has signed a Free Trade Agreement (FTA) with China. Fonterra is a big winner - gaining access to the massive Chinese market.
a Use the circular flow model to illustrate the impact of this FTA on rural economies.
b Fully the explain the impact on the wider economy over time.

ISBN: 9780170215718

Kiwi apple growers question report

JON MORGAN
Last updated 05:00 02/06/2011

New Zealand apple growers are casting doubt on a report that says apple prices will plummet in Australia when New Zealand apples arrive in the shops.

The report says that in just three years growers can expect their incomes to fall 32 per cent with imported apples securing almost a quarter of the market.

However, it will be a win for consumers, with prices going down on average 21 per cent.

The report says apples from New Zealand will be of the same high quality taste-wise, but will be 61 per cent cheaper, while US apples will cost 28 per cent less and Chinese apples 18 per cent less.

At the same time apple consumption will jump 17 per cent.

But Pipfruit NZ chief executive Peter Beaven said the report did not make sense. 'The size of the market it says we will have sounds greatly exaggerated to me.'

New Zealand expectations were that it would take time to grow the market to 500,000 cases a year, 5 per cent of the market.

Apple import protocols are being negotiated after a World Trade Organisation ruling last year that said Australian rules were too restrictive. Trade is expected to resume next year.

Source: businessday.co.nz

ISBN: 9780170215718

Growth

1 ▪ What is Growth?

> **By the end of this unit you will be able to:**
>
> - Explain what is meant by economic growth.
> - Explain three differing concepts of growth.
> - Illustrate each of the three different growth concepts using the Production Possibility Frontier model.

The issue of **growth** focuses on New Zealand's ability to improve the standards of living of its inhabitants. **Satisfying wants** is a fundamental principle of human behaviour in general, and of economics specifically. A nation's ability to satisfy the unlimited wants of its inhabitants is generally dependent on its ability to produce or acquire goods and services. Thus, growth is usually seen as the **increase in goods and services** or the **increase in production of goods and services**. Growth and economic development go hand in hand. Development is the ability to produce higher standards of living over time.

There are three different ways to define growth:

- Real income
- Productive capacity
- Net social welfare.

Real income

Real income refers to actual economic output, i.e. the number of goods and services produced by an economy. Using a simple circular flow model, it is easy to see that the output of an economy must equal the income of its households. This measure equates to Gross Domestic Product, which is explored further in the next unit.

ISBN: 9780170215718

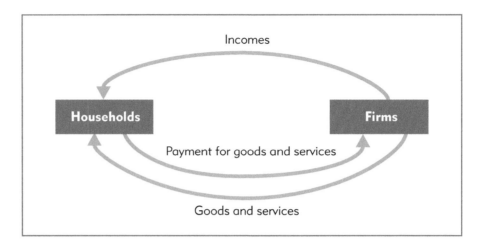

Productive capacity

This is a measure of an economy's **ability** to produce goods and services. Rather than looking at the actual output of an economy, the **potential** of the economy is assessed. The Organisation for Economic Co-operation and Development (OECD) measures 'economic potential' and compares it to actual performance in its 'output gaps' statistics.

Real Income

Here growth is seen to be an increase in output levels alone. An economy experiencing growth in output (and thus income) could be moving from a point inside the PPF to one closer to or on the frontier.

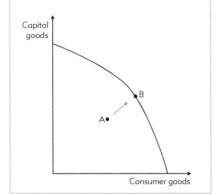

Productive Capacity

Here growth is seen to be an increase in potential output levels. The actual level of output is not necessarily changing. An economy experiencing growth in output potential must experience a shift of the PPF (but need not actually increase current output levels).

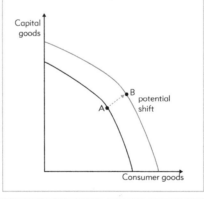

Net Social Welfare

Here growth is seen as improvements in both economic or output terms and in terms of non-economic factors. Economic growth could either be improving its resource use or taking advantage of actual increases in potential.

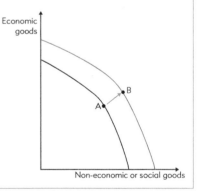

ISBN: 9780170215718

Net social welfare

This measure attempts to include 'quality of life' factors. As well as economic measures, which focus on the production of goods and services, it includes non-economic factors. These non-economic factors range from the concept of welfare to a consideration of the environment, or entertainment and facilities that may be provided by central government, such as health and education. One such measure that attempts this wider view is the Human Development Index (HDI).

HDI rank		Human Development Index (HDI) value	Life expectancy at birth (years)	Mean years of schooling (years)	Expected years of schooling (years)	Gross national income (GNI) per capita (PPP 2008 $)	GNI per capita rank minus HDI rank	Nonincome HDI value
		2010	2010	2010	2010[b]	2010	2010	2010
VERY HIGH HUMAN DEVELOPMENT								
1	Norway	**0.938**	81.0	12.6	17.3	58,810	2	0.954
2	Australia	**0.937**	81.9	12.0	20.5	38,692	11	0.989
3	New Zealand	**0.907**	80.6	12.5	19.7	25,438	30	0.979
4	United States	**0.902**	79.6	12.4	15.7	47,094	5	0.917
5	Ireland	**0.895**	80.3	11.6	17.9	33,078	20	0.936
6	Liechtenstein	**0.891**	79.6	10.3	14.8	81,011	−5	0.861
7	Netherlands	**0.890**	80.3	11.2	16.7	40,658	4	0.911
8	Canada	**0.888**	81.0	11.5	16.0	38,668	6	0.913
9	Sweden	**0.885**	81.3	11.6	15.6	36,936	8	0.911
10	Germany	**0.885**	80.2	12.2	15.6	35,308	9	0.915
11	Japan	**0.884**	83.2	11.5	15.1	34,692	11	0.915
12	Korea, Republic of	**0.877**	79.8	11.6	16.8	29,518	16	0.918
13	Switzerland	**0.874**	82.2	10.3	15.5	39,849	−1	0.889
HIGH HUMAN DEVELOPMENT								
43	Bahamas	**0.784**	74.4	11.1	11.6	25,201	−9	0.788
44	Lithuania	**0.783**	72.1	10.9	16.0	14,824	7	0.832
45	Chile	**0.783**	78.8	9.7	14.5	13,561	11	0.840
46	Argentina	**0.775**	75.7	9.3	15.5	14,603	6	0.821
47	Kuwait	**0.771**	77.9	6.1	12.5	55,719	−42	0.714
48	Latvia	**0.769**	73.0	10.4	15.4	12,944	13	0.822
49	Montenegro	**0.769**	74.6	10.6	14.4	12,491	16	0.825
50	Romania	**0.767**	73.2	10.6	14.8	12,844	13	0.820
51	Croatia	**0.767**	76.7	9.0	13.8	16,389	−2	0.798
52	Uruguay	**0.765**	76.7	8.4	15.7	13,808	3	0.810
53	Libyan Arab Jamahiriya	**0.755**	74.5	7.3	16.5	17,068	−5	0.775
54	Panama	**0.755**	76.0	9.4	13.5	13,347	4	0.796
55	Saudi Arabia	**0.752**	73.3	7.8	13.5	24,726	−20	0.742
MEDIUM HUMAN DEVELOPMENT								
86	Fiji	**0.669**	69.2	11.0	13.0	4,315	21	0.771
87	Turkmenistan	**0.669**	65.3	9.9	13.0	7,052	1	0.719
88	Dominican Republic	**0.663**	72.8	6.9	11.9	8,273	−9	0.695
89	China	**0.663**	73.5	7.5	11.4	7,258	−4	0.707
90	El Salvador	**0.659**	72.0	7.7	12.1	6,498	0	0.711
91	Sri Lanka	**0.658**	74.4	8.2	12.0	4,886	10	0.738
92	Thailand	**0.654**	69.3	6.6	13.5	8,001	−11	0.683
93	Gabon	**0.648**	61.3	7.5	12.7	12,747	−29	0.637
94	Suriname	**0.646**	69.4	7.2	12.0	7,093	−7	0.681
95	Bolivia, Plurinational State of	**0.643**	66.3	9.2	13.7	4,357	11	0.724
96	Paraguay	**0.640**	72.3	7.8	12.0	4,585	9	0.714
97	Philippines	**0.638**	72.3	8.7	11.5	4,002	12	0.726
98	Botswana	**0.633**	55.5	8.9	12.4	13,204	−38	0.613
LOW HUMAN DEVELOPMENT								
128	Kenya	**0.470**	55.6	7.0	9.6	1,628	10	0.541
129	Bangladesh	**0.469**	66.9	4.8	8.1	1,587	12	0.543
130	Ghana	**0.467**	57.1	7.1	9.7	1,385	14	0.556
131	Cameroon	**0.460**	51.7	5.9	9.8	2,197	−3	0.493
132	Myanmar	**0.451**	62.7	4.0	9.2	1,596	8	0.511
133	Yemen	**0.439**	63.9	2.5	8.6	2,387	−9	0.453
134	Benin	**0.435**	62.3	3.5	9.2	1,499	8	0.491
135	Madagascar	**0.435**	61.2	5.2	10.2	953	22	0.550
165	Mozambique	**0.284**	48.4	1.2	8.2	854	−5	0.300
166	Burundi	**0.282**	51.4	2.7	9.6	402	0	0.400
167	Niger	**0.261**	52.5	1.4	4.3	675	−3	0.285
168	Congo, Democratic Republic of the	**0.239**	48.0	3.8	7.8	291	0	0.390
169	Zimbabwe	**0.140**	47.0	7.2	9.2	176	0	0.472

ISBN: 9780170215718

Economics for NCEA Level 2

HDI rank	Human Development Index (HDI) value	Life expectancy at birth (years)	Mean years of schooling (years)	Expected years of schooling (years)	Gross national income (GNI) per capita (PPP 2008 $)	GNI per capita rank minus HDI rank	Nonincome HDI value
	2010	2010	2010	2010[b]	2010	2010	2010
Developed							
OECD	**0.879**	80.3	11.4	15.9	37,077	—	0.904
Non-OECD	**0.844**	80.0	10.0	13.9	42,370	—	0.845
Developing							
Arab States	**0.588**	69.1	5.7	10.8	7,861	—	0.610
East Asia and the Pacific	**0.643**	72.6	7.2	11.5	6,403	—	0.692
Europe and Central Asia	**0.702**	69.5	9.2	13.6	11,462	—	0.740
Latin America and the Caribbean	**0.704**	74.0	7.9	13.7	10,642	—	0.746
South Asia	**0.516**	65.1	4.6	10.0	3,417	—	0.551
Sub-Saharan Africa	**0.389**	52.7	4.5	9.0	2,050	—	0.436
Very high human development	**0.878**	80.3	11.3	15.9	37,225	—	0.902
High human development	**0.717**	72.6	8.3	13.8	12,286	—	0.749
Medium human development	**0.592**	69.3	6.3	11.0	5,134	—	0.634
Low human development	**0.393**	56.0	4.1	8.2	1,490	—	0.445
Least developed countries	**0.386**	57.7	3.7	8.0	1,393	—	0.441
World	**0.624**	69.3	7.4	12.3	10,631	—	0.663

Sri Lanka manages a life expectancy of 74 years and an adult literacy rate of 87% with a per capita income of just $5000. By contrast, Brazil has a life expectancy of 72 years, and its adult literacy rate is 73% at a per capita income of $10 800. In Saudi Arabia, where the per capita income is $24 800, life expectancy is only 73 years and the adult literacy rate is an estimated 55%.

What matters is how economic growth is managed and distributed for the benefit of the people.

Many countries are developing systems for measuring more than a purely economic measure of well-being. Australia, Bhutan, Canada, UK and New Zealand have recently developed other measures.

Treasury into 'science of happiness'

Andrea Vance

They say economists know the price of everything and the value of nothing – but the Treasury has gone cuddly and is now focusing on living standards.

The Government's chief policy adviser will now measure happiness, trust and the value of leisure in a bid to provide ministers with "more robust" guidance.

Treasury Secretary John Whitehead announced the new direction yesterday, in his last public speech before he steps down next week.

He said the department – a "central agency" in the public sector – was often criticised for concentrating on income and gross domestic product as a measure of the country's wellbeing.

GDP and gross national income "are not all that matters", he said. "Treasury certainly cares about more than just growth.

While a well-performing economy is one of the key drivers of higher living standards, and advising on how to improve economic performance is one of our core roles, we recognise that there are a broad range of factors that contribute to New Zealanders' lives."

The Working Towards Higher Living Standards framework was unveiled on the same day as the OECD released its interactive Better Life Index to allow people to measure their wellbeing – but officials said this was a coincidence.

Source: *The Dominion Post*

ISBN: 9780170215718

ACTIVITY

1 Define growth.
2 Explain the difference between each of the three measures of growth.
3 Explain why the real output measure may be considered inadequate for measuring a standard of living.
4 Using this table, rank each of the countries for each of the categories (1= the best and 9 = the worst) on a copy of the table below. Use the extra column to add the country's score across all categories except GDP.

**Be careful: Literacy rates that are high are GOOD.
Infant mortality rates that are high are BAD.**

Country	GDP per capita (2005 PPP US$)	Literacy rate %	Life expectancy at birth	Under 5 mortality/ 1000	Public expenditure on health as % of GDP	Public expenditure on the military as % of GDP	Seats in parliament held by women %
Norway	58 278	99	81	4	7.5	1.9	62
Vietnam	3097	90.3	74.9	14	2.8	2.5	34.7
New Zealand	27 520	99	80.6	6	7.1	1	50.6
Costa Rica	11 143	96.3	79.1	11	5.9	.6	58.3
Malaysia	14 410	92.9	74.7	6	1.9	2.0	16.4
USA	46 653	na	79.6	8	7.1	4.06	19.9
Zimbabwe	187	92.6	47	96	4.1	3.8	25.8
Brazil	10 847	72.9	72.9	22	3.5	1.7	10.2
Samoa	4260	98.8	72.2	26	4.2	-	.9

Country	GDP per capita (2005 PPP US$)	Literacy rate %	Life expectancy at birth	Under 5 mortality/ 1000	Public expenditure on health as % of GDP	Public expenditure on the military as % of GDP	Seats in parliament held by women %	Rankings
Norway								
Vietnam								
New Zealand								
Costa Rica								
Malaysia								
USA								
Zimbabwe								
Brazil								
Samoa								

ISBN: 9780170215718

2 ▪ Calculating GDP

By the end of this unit you will be able to:

- Define GDP.
- Calculate GDP using the expenditure, income and value added approaches.
- Relate these approaches to the simple circular flow model.

Economic figures about the rate of growth of the New Zealand economy are based upon the **Gross Domestic Production** (GDP) produced by Statistics New Zealand. GDP measures the value of all final goods and services produced by an economy in one year, measured in current or market prices. As the value of production is measured in market (or current) prices, it will be affected by inflation.

Measuring Gross Domestic Product

GDP is a nominal figure. **Nominal** means in current prices. When the distorting effect of price changes has been removed, the figures are referred to as inflation adjusted or **real**.

A simple circular flow model is useful in illustrating the concepts behind GDP. In this model the producers make goods and services and the consumers buy the output. There are no *leakages* in the two-sector economy, so we also know that the payments made for goods and services by households to firms is equal to the value of all the goods and services produced in the economy (flow **3**). Also, these two amounts must equal the payments the firms make for use of the resources, i.e. flow **1** = flow **2**.

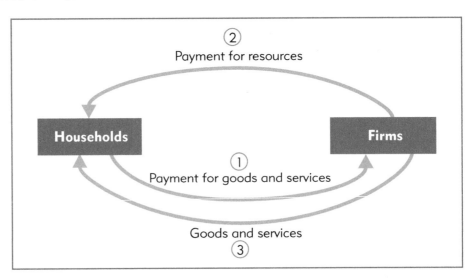

ISBN: 9780170215718

Keeping these ideas in mind we can see that there are three methods we could use to determine GDP.

1 Calculate the value of the goods and services produced (flow **3**) by adding the costs of the firms involved in the production of those goods and services. This method is called the **Production** or **Value Added method** or **Value added approach**.

2 Calculate the value of the income earned by households (flow **2**). This flow is equal to flow **3** (and must therefore also equal the value of the goods and services produced). This method is called the **Income method** or **Income approach**.

3 Calculate the value of the goods and services by measuring the amount households have spent on those goods and services (flow **1**). This method is called the **Expenditure method** or **Expenditure approach**.

1 Explain how economic activity can be measured by the flow of incomes or the flow of payments for goods and services.

2 Describe the difference between savings and investment.

3 Explain how increased investment will lead to economic growth.

4 Describe the difference between an injection into the circular flow and a withdrawal from the circular flow.

5 Identify four withdrawals from a five-sector circular flow model.

6 Identify three injections in a five-sector circular flow model.

PRODUCTION APPROACH

To calculate this, Statistics New Zealand collects data via surveys from local businesses. The businesses are grouped by industry. The value of **gross** (total) **output** of each industry is calculated. The **intermediate consumption** in each industry is also calculated. This is the value of intermediate goods produced and then used by or sold to other firms to use in the production of the final good or service. These two figures (gross and intermediate) give an estimate of the **value added** by the industry. The value added by each of the industries is summed to give the overall figure for GDP. A very simplified picture of the production approach is shown below.

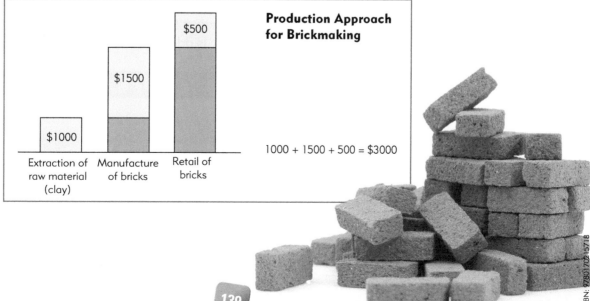

Production Approach for Brickmaking

$500

$1500

$1000

Extraction of raw material (clay)   Manufacture of bricks   Retail of bricks

1000 + 1500 + 500 = $3000

ISBN: 9780170215718

INCOME APPROACH

This method measures GDP as the **sum** of all incomes earned by households for the use of the factors of production (resources). To calculate GDP using this method, Statistics New Zealand could use data collected from employees (salaries and wages), businesses (profits) and government (indirect taxes).

The terminology used comes from the New Zealand System of National Accounts (NZSNA), which outlines, among other things, how GDP is to be calculated. This system is based upon an internationally accepted standard developed by the United Nations.

	Compensation of Employees (salaries and wages)
plus	Gross Operating Surplus (profits + an allowance for depreciation of assets)
plus	Net Indirect Taxes (taxes on production and imports minus subsidies)
equals	GDP

EXPENDITURE APPROACH

The expenditure approach measures the value of *all purchases* of all final goods and services produced in the economy (intermediate goods are excluded). Obviously the New Zealand economy is not a simple two-sector economy and the purchases made by all sectors must be accounted for. For example:

- For households all consumption (C) must be accounted for
- For the firms we calculate investment (I)
- Spending by government (G)
- Spending by overseas countries on goods and services produced in New Zealand, i.e. exports (X)
- Less the spending by New Zealand on goods and services produced overseas, i.e. imports (M)

The formula is:

(X - M) is called net exports

$$\textbf{GDP (expenditure approach)} = \textbf{C} + \textbf{I} + \textbf{G} + \textbf{(X - M)}$$

Again, the NZSNA has a terminology all of its own for each of these groups.

	C	Final Consumption Expenditure (Private or Households)
plus	I	Gross Fixed Capital Formation
plus	G	Final Consumption Expenditure (Public or Government)
plus	X	Exports
minus	M	Imports
equals		GDP

Each method of calculating GDP should give the same result but the difficulties of collecting precise data means this is rarely achieved. To make sure they do equal, a statistical discrepancy is added to the expenditure method:

income approach = expenditure approach + statistical discrepancy

ISBN: 9780170215718

ISBN: 9780170215718

ACTIVITY

1 Decide whether each of these transactions would be a withdrawal or an injection in the circular flow model, then explain how it would impact upon economic activity and why.

   a Fonterra experiences record profit levels.
   b New Zealand experiences an export-led boom.
   c Government agrees to increases in social welfare spending.
   d GST rates increase to 15%.
   e New motorways built in Auckland.
   f Consumers spend up at Christmas.
   g The forestry industry plants new forests.
   h New Zealand imports more secondhand cars following new regulations.
   i The last remaining subsidies are phased out in accordance with international trade agreements.
   j Fonterra builds a modern milk-processing plan in Southland.
   k Imports of oil rise.
   l Subsidies are offered to film production companies.

2 Illustrate the differences between the production, expenditure and income methods of calculating GDP using the circular flow model.

3 Use the figures provided to calculate GDP for 2009 and 2010.

	2009 ($m)	2010 ($m)
Net Indirect Taxes	22 137	-
Gross Operating Surplus	79 857	80 195
Final Consumption Expenditure — Private	108 602	110 834
Compensation of Employees	83 567	84 486
Final Consumption Expenditure — Public	37 265	38 213
Net Exports	-2401	-
Gross Fixed Capital Formation	40 315	36 845
Taxes on Production and Imports	-	23 775
Subsidies	-	654
Imports	-	49 690
Exports	-	52 424
Statistical Discrepancy	582	501

Note: *Statistics New Zealand* is currently progressively implementing ANZSIC06 into its economic statistics. This will be completed by the release of New Zealand National Accounts in 2011, and tourism satellite accounts and productivity statistics in 2012.

New Zealand will consider adopting the SNA08 and BPM6 changes, subject to the availability of resources including funding, no earlier than 2013. It is understood that this timeframe is similar to, if not earlier than, those currently suggested by the European Union, USA and Canadian statistical offices.

3 ▪ Real GDP and Real GDP per capita

By the end of this unit you will be able to:

- Define Real GDP.
- Explain the GDP deflator and use it to calculate Real GDP.
- Calculate and explain Real GDP per capita.
- Outline the limitations of GDP statistics.
- Outline a range of alternative statistics for measuring standards of living.

GDP figures include the effects of inflation. It is important to remove the distortion of price changes to get a better picture of growth. Real GDP (RGDP) is nominal GDP adjusted for inflation. It measures the value of all final goods and services produced by an economy in one year measured in **constant prices**. While this is a more useful figure than nominal GDP, it is still not useful for comparing international growth and output. RGDP can be adjusted for population size giving RGDP *per capita* (or per person). RGDP per capita best compares to the real income idea introduced in an earlier unit. It is a recognised measure for standards of living as well.

GDP and growth

GDP figures alone are not useful for measuring growth because they include changes in prices as well as output.

> GDP essentially measures the price of each good or service bought by households multiplied by the quantity of the goods or services bought by the households.
>
> $$GDP = P \times Q$$
>
> The definition also ensures we are referring to one year's production and that same year's prices.
>
> $$GDP = P_{year1} \times Q_{year1}$$
>
> Thus any increase in GDP could be the result of an increase in price, or an increase in output, or an increase in both. It is impossible to tell from the figure itself.

ISBN: 9780170215718

Real GDP removes the distortion caused by increasing prices.

$$RGDP = GDP \text{ adjusted for prices} = \frac{P_{year1} \times Q_{year1}}{P_{year1}} \times P_{base\ year}$$

The original price level is removed (they cancel) and the constant price level is used instead.

We know from our work with inflation that the price level is measured using the CPI statistics so we can rewrite this formula as:

$$RGDP = \frac{GDP_{year1} \times CPI_{base}}{CPI_{year1}} \qquad OR \qquad RGDP = GDP_{year1} \times \frac{CPI_{base}}{CPI_{year1}}$$

$$\text{The GDP deflator is: } \frac{CPI_{base}}{CPI_{year1}}$$

A worked example of calculating RGDP

Year	Nominal GDP ($m)	CPI (base year 1989)
1989	91 548	1000
1999	97 654	1053

RGDP 1989 = nominal GDP in 1989 as it is the base year.

RGDP 1999 $= \dfrac{97\ 654}{1} \times \dfrac{1000}{1053}$

= $92 738.84 M

In order to compare different-sized populations, RGDP figures are adjusted to create RGDP per capita.

$$RGDP \text{ per capita} = \frac{RGDP}{population}$$

This enables the GDP figures for countries as different as China and the United States to be compared meaningfully with New Zealand's data.

ISBN: 9780170215718

Economics for NCEA Level 2

ACTIVITY

Use the information provided below to calculate:
- **a** The GDP deflator for the years 2008–2010.
- **b** RGDP for the years 2008–2010.
- **c** RGDP per capita for the years 2008–2010.

Estimated population of New Zealand 2003–2010	
2003	4 061 600
2004	4 114 300
2005	4 161 000
2006	4 211 400
2007	4 252 600
2008	4 291 600
2009	4 347 200
2010 P	4 393 500

GDP in current prices $(million)	
2003	132 425
2004	141 702
2005	151 700
2006	160 273
2007	168 328
2008	181 020
2009	184 168
2010	187 362

CPI (base = 1000)	
2003	924
2004	949
2005	979
2006	1005
2007	1037
2008	1072
2009	1093
2010 P	1137

Limitations of the GDP statistics

It is important to remember that the GDP statistics have several shortcomings.

Non-market activities are not included

All unpaid activity is excluded (more accurately it is *not included*).

- Subsistence economies, where the producer essentially consumes all production as there is no surplus to sell, will have GDP figures that understate their standard of living. This is because the producer's output is never sold in the market.
- Housework and volunteer work is excluded. Again this means GDP figures understate standards of living. Another criticism of this is that females predominantly perform these functions and thus the statistics typically recognise male input into an economy but not female input.
- The black economy or illegal activity (including 'under the table' payments) is not included. The Aotearoa Legalise Cannabis Party quoted 'The Northland economy's earnings alone from trade in the illicit substance has just been

ISBN: 9780170215718

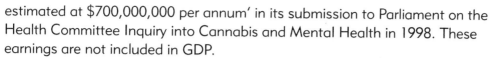

estimated at $700,000,000 per annum' in its submission to Parliament on the Health Committee Inquiry into Cannabis and Mental Health in 1998. These earnings are not included in GDP.

- Any barter transactions and private sales, for example garage sales, are also excluded.

Negative vs positive production

- There is no indication in the statistics whether the economic activity was positive or negative. When there are major oil spills, such as the *Rena* running aground on a reef off the coast of Tauranga in 2011, and huge salvage and clean-up operations, these activities will boost national income. Is this an increase in living standards?
- There is no indication that the quality of life has improved. Longer working hours and less leisure time may result in greater output but arguably lower standards of living.
- There is no indication of whether the national income is going towards defence rather than education or health.

Income distribution

- There is no indication in these statistics of how the national income is shared among the population.

> **Alternatives to GDP**
> We have already considered the HDI but others include:
> - Environmental statistics
> - Employment statistics
> - Household income and outlay
> - Time use survey.

Photo by Mark Elstone

ISBN: 9780170215718

4 ■ The Role of Investment

By the end of this unit you will be able to:

- Demonstrate how investment (both physical and human), technology and resource expansion contribute to growth.
- Illustrate, using a Production Possibility Frontier, the opportunity cost of present consumption in terms of future growth.

We return to the concepts of *growth*. The Production Possibility Frontier model is able to illustrate these ideas further. It can illustrate the determinants (or causes) of growth, focusing primarily on the role of investment. Investment has a very specific meaning in Economics. It means an increase in man-made resources (capital). These man-made resources are very significant with respect to economic growth.

Resources and investment and the PPF revisited

In an earlier unit we saw that resources are the inputs into the production process.

| INPUTS
Resources
Factors of Production | → | PRODUCTION
PROCESS | → | OUTPUTS
Goods and Services |

Resources are classified into human, natural and man-made resources. In the PPF model these resources are fixed. The only way in which an economy is able to produce a greater maximum output level is if the resources are increased in some way or the methods used to transform the resources into goods and services (technology) improve. Investment is the term given to increases in man-made resources (capital).

The determinants of growth

Increasing productive capacity or potential will only come about if:

1 The quantity or quality of human resources are increased by:
  - Increases in general population through natural increase or immigration.
  - Increases in working population through changes in social attitudes to work.
  - Increased quality of human resources through education or through improved management and workplace practices (technological improvement).

> Education is also called *investment in human capital*.

Capital, or man-made resources, is defined as any input into a productive process that has had human effort applied to it. As most workers are now educated and trained, they are now referred to as human capital.

ISBN: 9780170215718

2 New natural resources are discovered.

3 There is increased production of man-made resources, that is, increased investment.

> Investment is also called *capital formation*.

1 Copy and complete the following diagram.

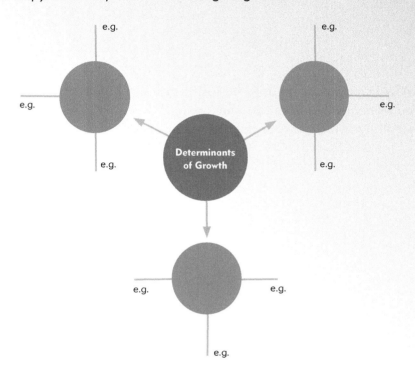

2

Downgrade highlights need for repairs

By Susan Guthrie and Gareth Morgan

Property speculation is the national pastime and with that obsession we have missed the opportunity to use the vast imports of overseas capital to develop a robust economic base. Instead we have run up a large external debt to fund this tit-for-tat escalation of each other's house values. Building more and more houses as part of playing this game can hardly be regarded as a credible growth strategy.

a Explain why Guthrie and Morgan believe 'building more and more houses cannot be regarded as a credible growth strategy'.

b Explain the phrase 'vast imports of overseas capital'.

c Outline a more growth oriented use of those overseas funds instead of using them for housing.

d Explain why some argue for a capital gains tax (a tax on the increased value of houses) on housing to help stimulate a more productive use of overseas capital.

ISBN: 9780170215718

Economics for NCEA Level 2

5 ▪ Growth and the AS/AD Economic Model

By the end of this unit you will be able to:

- Apply the AS/AD model to illustrate growth concepts.
- Apply the AS/AD model to analyse growth concepts.

The AS/AD Model

The AS/AD model can be used to illustrate growth concepts.

You will remember from the inflation topic that the AS/AD model is a representation of the total or aggregate economy.

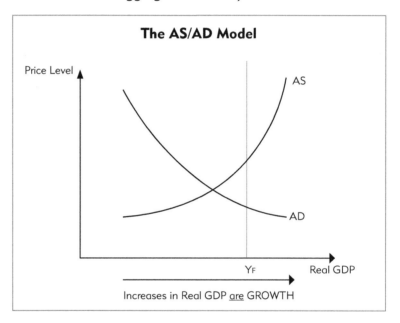

The AS/AD Model

On the vertical axis we have the price level — an aggregate measure of all prices in the economy. On the horizontal axis we have Real GDP — total output of an economy in a year measured in constant prices.

Increases in Real GDP are growth. By analysing changes in the economy it is possible to see the effect on growth.

A recap of the factors that affect aggregate demand (AD) and aggregate supply (AS) is given below. (Review pages 35–6 for more detail.)

AD is affected by changes in:

- (C) Household spending, which is affected by interest rates, disposable incomes, inflationary expectations and consumer confidence.
- (I) Investment spending by firms is affected by interest rates and business confidence.
- (G) Government spending is affected by a change in government policy.
- (X - M) Net exports are affected by exchange rates, which in turn are affected by interest rates, and changes in overseas demand.

ISBN: 9780170215718

AS is affected by changes in:

- Nominal wages.
- Productivity.
- Import costs of imported raw materials.

Let's consider the effect of rising oil prices on Real GDP.

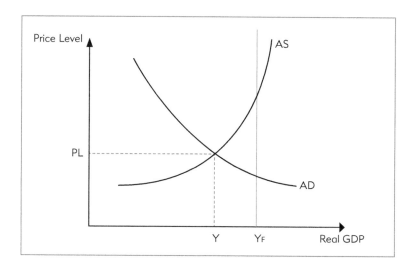

The economy represented above is operating at the equilibrium price level PL and the equilibrium output level Y.

Rising oil prices are an **imported raw material**. They will cause costs of production to rise for firms, so AS will decrease. This is shown in the graph below as a shift to the left of the AS curve.

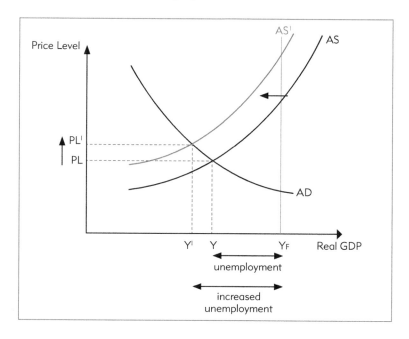

This has caused a rise in the general level of prices, the cost-push inflation we saw in the inflation unit.

It has also caused a fall in real GDP to Y^I. The output produced by firms has fallen. This is a contraction of the economy. There is less growth.

It is also possible, if you have studied employment, to look at the impact of this fall in output on employment levels. Fewer workers will be required as less output is being made, so we would anticipate a rise in unemployment.

ISBN: 9780170215718

Economics for NCEA Level 2

1

New Zealand consumer spending down

New Zealand consumer spending fell for the first time in three months in July.

a Using the AD/AS model of the New Zealand economy, illustrate the effect a fall in consumer spending would have on Real GDP.

b Give a detailed explanation of the changes you have made.

2

Christchurch earthquake to prompt OCR cut, says ASB economist

An ASB Bank economist says she expects Reserve Bank governor Alan Bollard to cut the official cash rate in part due to the economic impact of the Christchurch earthquake.

a Using the AD/AS model of the New Zealand economy, illustrate the effect a fall in the OCR would have on Real GDP.

b Give a detailed explanation of the changes you have made.

3

Dairy helps boost export price index to record level

a Using the AD/AS model of the New Zealand economy, illustrate the effect a rise in exports would have on Real GDP.

b Give a detailed explanation of the changes you have made.

4

NZ exchange rate hits all-time high

a Using the AD/AS model of the New Zealand economy illustrate the effect a rise in the exchange rate would have on Real GDP.

b Give a detailed explanation of the changes you have made.

ISBN: 9780170215718

The PPF and investment

The Production Possibility Frontier model can illustrate a further growth concept:
The impact of low investment levels on present and future consumption.

The goods on the axes are **consumer goods** and **capital goods**. Consumer
goods are used by households and are indicative of **current standards of living**.
The capital goods are the man-made resources that are produced now and are
thus available to make more goods (either capital or consumer goods) in the
future.

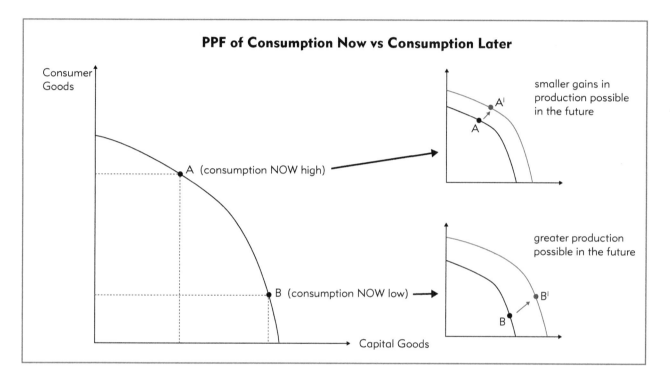

Higher consumption NOW – higher standards of living NOW.
The opportunity cost of producing consumer goods is foregoing capital goods.
If an economy is currently choosing to have a high consumption of consumer
goods then the economy is foregoing greater capital goods. The opportunity
cost of producing consumer goods is missing out on producing capital goods.
The ability to produce future consumer goods is reduced because the stock of
capital goods produced will be smaller than if we had chosen lower consumer
goods levels and higher capital good levels.

Lower consumption NOW – lower standards of living NOW.
The opportunity cost of producing consumer goods is foregoing capital goods.
If an economy is currently choosing to have a lower consumption of consumer
goods then the economy is foregoing fewer capital goods. The opportunity
cost of producing consumer goods is missing out on producing capital goods.
The ability to produce future consumer goods is increased because the
stock of capital goods produced will be smaller than if we had chosen higher
consumer goods levels and lower capital good levels.

ISBN: 9780170215718

Economics for NCEA Level 2

ACTIVITY

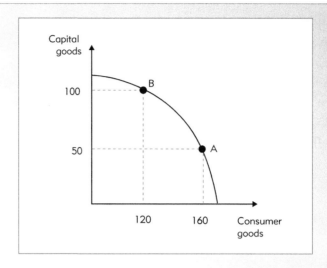

1 a Explain which position on the PPF above is most likely to result in future growth in New Zealand.
   b Calculate the opportunity cost of moving from Point **A** to Point **B**.
   c Explain whether or not high levels of savings equate to high standards of living now or in the future.

2 a Explain which point on the PPF below will result in a higher standard of living now.
   b Explain which point on the PPF will result in a lower standard of living in the future.

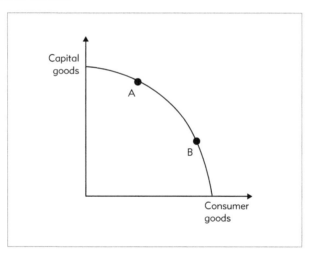

3 Historically New Zealand has had very low saving rates, i.e. New Zealanders spend most of their income NOW. Explain the effect that this will have on our standard of living now and in the future.

4 Kiwisaver has seen the development of greater investment funds available in New Zealand.
   a Illustrate the long term effect of those investment funds on New Zealand's economy using a PPF model.
   b Compare and contrast the standards of living of New Zealanders now and in the future following the introduction of Kiwisaver.

ISBN: 9780170215718

6 ▪ More on Investment

By the end of this unit you will be able to:

- Explain the major determinants of investment.
- Show the relationship between technology and productivity.

Unit 4 showed that **investment** is a key to growth. In this unit the major determinants of investment — the reasons why firms invest — are explored. The role of technology in growth and development is very much at the forefront of global economics. Technology is an improvement in method. The link between **technology** and **productivity** is outlined. **Productivity** is the measure of output per unit of input per time period. Increases in productivity mean that firms are able to increase output from the same resources. This will mean there is the opportunity for further growth.

Determinants of investment

The main factors firms consider when deciding to invest are:

1 Business confidence.
2 Costs involved in the investment. ⎫ These factors are interrelated.
3 Profitability of the investment. ⎭

The level of savings in an economy also impacts on investment levels.

Business confidence

This is a measure of how firms view the future. If they expect a positive outlook for their business, then business confidence is high; if they expect the economic situation for their firm to worsen, then business confidence is low. A wide of range of influences affect business confidence. It is a perception on the part of the firm as to where the economy is headed. Not everything is rational and business confidence, or the lack of it, can be self-fulfilling.

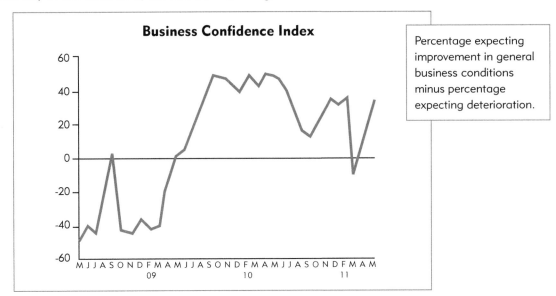

Business Confidence Index

Percentage expecting improvement in general business conditions minus percentage expecting deterioration.

ISBN: 9780170215718

Costs of investment

From our circular flow model we can see that firms borrow to finance investment.

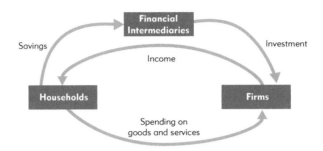

The cost of borrowing — interest rates — will affect the firm's decision to invest. Any increases in interest rates mean that borrowing is more expensive and thus the investment is more expensive.

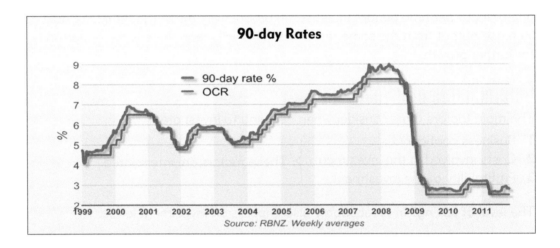

Profitability

Firms aim to increase profits through investment. Thus they must consider expected revenues following investment against the costs of investment. Therefore the expected outlook (business confidence) and the costs of investment (interest rates) combine to give an expected profitabilty of investment.

Level of savings

The circular flow model illustrates the link between investment and savings. The funds that firms use to finance investment are the savings of households. The **National Disposable Income** measures the income available to New Zealand residents for **current consumption** (spending) or **saving**.

Technology and productivity

Technology is an improvement in method. If methods improve, more output from the same resources is possible. Improved technology leads to greater productivity. While we tend to think of technology as increased use of machinery, particularly increased use of computers, it can be much more simple than that. New materials, new ideas and innovative production processes are all examples of technology.

ISBN: 9780170215718

1 Explain the effect of:
   a Increased savings on investment.
   b Increased research and development on investment.
   c Increased investment on productivity.

2 Explain the effect of:
   a Increased investment on growth.
   b Increased investment on international competitiveness.
   c Increased investment on employment.

Use the article below to answer questions **3** to **6**.

3 Explain the acronym R & D.

4 Explain the link between R & D and growth.

5 Use the AS/AD model to illustrate this link.

6 R & D tax credits are available to New Zealand firms. Using the article below, explain how this scheme would increase innovation and develop new export products.

Budget 2011: Little hope of R&D increase

By Hamish Fletcher

Many industry commentators did not want to speak publicly about what the Government will do but indicated it was unlikely to put more into research and development spending. Those who did offer a forecast were pessimistic about funding increases.

The MacDiarmid Institute's deputy director Shaun Hendy said public spending in science and technology was tipped to remain static.

"I don't think it will be a great Budget for science, but I don't think it's going to be a potentially disastrous Budget either," he said.

However, while spending might not be cut, Hendy said increasing funding was an essential part of boosting high-value exports.

"Both our government R&D spending and our business R&D spending is pretty tragic, both in terms of our percentage of GDP and in absolutes. A lot of the work I've done shows that you get what you pay for. If you want a high-tech, export-based economy then you actually need to put both public and private sector money into it and we haven't had a Budget in my lifetime that's actually addressed that."

Hendy said the high-tech sector would need to grow fives times bigger if the Government is serious about closing the gap with the Australian economy.

"One of the things we certainly need [to close the gap] is a high performing advanced manufacturing sector and we probably need to multiply the number of people working in the sector by five - that's something that other countries have done," he said.

Xero's general manager of finance Paul Williams agreed there was little hope tomorrow's announcement would give more funding to the tech sector.

"At this stage we're not really expecting anything to come out because the Government tends to give a heads up of a lot of the things that are in the Budget," he said.

Williams said the Government would be wise to put more into developing this part of the economy.

"We've got so much potential and throwing money at the high-tech industry certainly makes a lot of sense."

NZICT chief executive Brett O'Riley said the sector also has to play a part in encouraging public money.

CONT. OVER

ISBN: 9780170215718

Economics for NCEA Level 2

ISBN: 9780170215718

ACTIVITY

"The Government has quite clearly signalled, that their goal is to increase R&D spending over time on a per capita basis, but I think we need to develop some proof points around the expenditure in last year's Budget to justify the increase."

Williams said the problem for the Government was working out which businesses would be able to turn funding into export dollars.

"How do you actually target the money in the most efficient way?"

The OECD Economic Survey of New Zealand 2011 suggests a number of different strategies for lifting growth rates in New Zealand.

Economic Survey of New Zealand 2011

1 **The recovery stalled in 2010, despite record terms of trade and support from policy stimulus.** Households, businesses and farmers are attempting to repair over-extended balance sheets in the aftermath of a property boom. The effects of two damaging earthquakes will further retard the recovery and make the outlook highly uncertain.

2 **The recession has highlighted the need for structural reforms.** With the property boom of the past decade financed by private sector borrowing from abroad through the banking system, net foreign liabilities have accumulated to levels that make the economy vulnerable to sharp changes in investor sentiment. The economy now faces the challenge of a combination of high external deficits and international debt, an overvalued exchange rate, a heavy cost of capital and unbalanced growth.

3 **Achieving faster growth will require progress across a broad policy front.** This includes bolder fiscal consolidation in the form of spending restraint, coupled with tax and pension reforms to boost national saving. These measures would allow interest rates to stay low for longer and create room for the exchange rate to ease, thereby facilitating the needed rebalancing of the economy, boosting output of tradable goods and services.

4 **Favourable tax treatment of housing and inefficient regulatory constraints on supply should be removed.** These distortions exaggerated the surge in house prices, giving rise to wider wealth inequalities and a heavy dependence of households' long term financial positions on volatile property values. Policy priorities should include further tax reforms to level the playing field for saving and investment decisions, while improving the efficiency of land use policies and the overall urban planning system.

5 **Regaining regulatory best practice and improving management of the government's considerable asset holdings could help boost productivity growth.** New Zealand's long standing front runner status in product market regulation has been eroded over the past decade. Regulatory governance should be further fortified to improve the overall investment environment, while moving towards full or even partial privatisation of state controlled commercial assets would strengthen market discipline and transparency.

6 **Green growth would help to consolidate New Zealand's long run growth potential.** As an exporter of resource based goods and services, its 'brand' relies on the environmental integrity of its output and policies. The Emissions Trading Scheme is a major development, but market based instruments to give natural assets a value should be used more broadly, notably to allocate water efficiently.

ISBN: Growth

From paragraph 1

7 Outline the significant factors causing the economy to struggle in 2011.

8 Using the AS/AD model, show the impact these factors had on our economy.

From paragraph 3

9 Outline the two major areas of concern the report identifies with regard to growth.

10 Using the AS/AD model, show the impact of each of these two factors on our economy.

From paragraph 6

11 Explain what is meant by New Zealand's 'green' brand.

12 Explain the effect that damage to our brand would have on our growth.

13 Illustrate your answer using the AS/AD model.

14 Compare and contrast the effect that low levels of household saving and damage to our 'brand' would have on New Zealand growth rates.

ISBN: 9780170215718

Economics for NCEA Level 2

7 ▪ The Impacts of Growth

By the end of this unit you will be able to:

- Explore the impacts of growth both positive and negative.
- Understand that these impacts are not evenly experienced by all groups in New Zealand society.

Growth has both positive and negative effects. The impacts of these effects are not evenly spread across all members of the global or national economy. Indeed those who experience the gains are not likely to also experience the losses, making the inherent inequality even greater. There is often a trade-off between economic growth (and increases in material standards of living) and a decline in the quality of our environment. In addition there is a growing gap between rich and poor within New Zealand and across many nations of the world.

Positive effects of growth

Growth and economic development are the primary measures of increases in living standards.

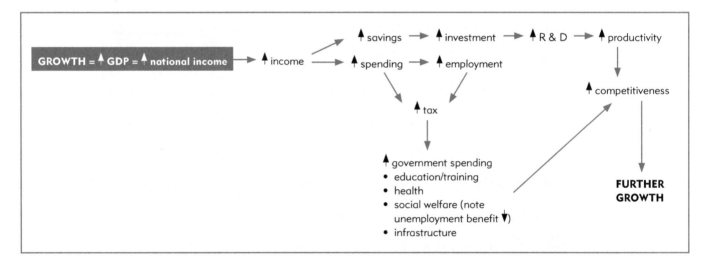

Negative effects of growth

Growth involves the use of resources. By not planning for the future, many resources have been threatened by overuse.

1 **Resource depletion:** Natural resources are particularly vulnerable to overuse, especially where ownership of the resource is unclear and no one takes responsibility for its continued care and management (e.g. deep-sea fishing). The Brazilian rainforest is an example of the dangers of growth — large-scale tree-felling threatens animals, plants and native inhabitants. As well, there are wider implications for the planet because of the vital role forests and jungles play in converting carbon dioxide (CO_2) into oxygen.

2 **Pollution:** Most production processes pollute. Consumption in the developed world also creates pollution and little responsibility for this pollution is taken by

ISBN: 9780170215718

the polluters. Global environmental problems associated with pollution include global warming, rising sea levels, holes in the ozone layer and acid rain.

3 Impact on society: Growth brings a breakdown in traditional ways of life, urbanisation, exploitation of the least developed nations, increasing industrial diseases (e.g. heart disease, stress and drug dependency). Terrorist attacks also draw attention to the pressures of life in the 'have not' economies and the implications of this for the 'haves'.

The world's response

The world is responding to the problems of growth, but slowly. Some recent initiatives are:

1 OECD World Summit on **Sustainable Development**
2 Kyoto Protocol
3 Southern Oceans Marine Reserve
4 Consumer rejection of drift-net tuna fishing and battery hens. (However it is arguable that only consumers in developed countries can afford to protest against these activities.)

Choose one of the four initiatives above (or another you are interested in — check with your teacher). Outline the initiative. Find out how successful your chosen initiative has been in minimising the negative impacts of growth. You will need to use your own paper for this research activity.

New Zealand's response

In New Zealand, efforts have been made to incorporate environmental and societal concerns into the planning process for new initiatives. The piece of legislation responsible for this is the **Resource Management Act (RMA) 1991**.

Environmental planning framework

The Resource Management Act 1991 facilitates planning of use, distribution or preservation of natural and physical resources. These resources include rivers, lakes, coastal and geothermal areas; land, including soils, forests and farmlands; the air; and the constructed environment — buildings, bridges and other structures in cities and towns.

The Act places emphasis on the effect a proposed activity will or might have on the environment, and encourages community involvement.

The purpose is to promote the sustainable management of natural and physical resources. The Act covers national policies, sustainable management, regional policies and plans, district planning, resource consents, public involvement in resource management, use of land, and waste management.

Source: *Statistics New Zealand*

ISBN: 9780170215718

Uneven impact of growth

Growth is not experienced evenly across New Zealand. **Annual growth rates for New Zealand do not reflect an across-the-board rise in all New Zealanders' standards of living.**

Inequalities between rich and poor are likely to be exacerbated by growth as the richer members of society take advantage of investment opportunities and an occupational and geographical mobility not available to the poorer members of society.

Don Brash: RMA is biggest obstacle

Tuesday Aug 9, 2011

…..The biggest obstacle to infrastructure development is the Resource Management Act.

We support the provisions in the Resource Management Act that provide for expedited consent processes for projects of national significance. ….

…..Act is concerned that New Zealand's water resources are not being used optimally and that our water infrastructure leaves much to be desired. Tradable water markets have created exceptional efficiency gains in Australia and should be given serious consideration in New Zealand.

1 **a** Outline the ACT Party's political philosophy.

   b Explain why Don Brash believes the RMA is the 'biggest obstacle to infrastructure development'.

The Green Party is calling for Maori rights under the Resource Management Act (RMA) to be protected.

Under proposed changes to the RMA, Maori will have their right to appeal council plans restricted. For example, if a council allows sewage discharge over kai moana beds, Maori will no longer have a right to appeal, said Green Party Maori Spokesperson Metiria Turei.

2 **a** Outline the Green Party's political philosophy.

   b Explain how the proposed changes will affect Maori interests in developments.

   c Explain how the proposed changes will impact other community members affected by developments.

   d Compare and contrast the views of the Green and Act parties.

8 ▪ The Government and Growth

There has been a major shift in approach in New Zealand regarding growth. Rather than being seen as the inevitable end result of improved economic performance in the areas of trade, price stability and employment, growth is now a specific goal in itself.

Supply side policies (for example, deregulation)

A philosophical change regarding the role of government occurred in the 1980s. This shift was arguably brought about by economic necessity. New Zealand was in desperate straits — successive budget deficits and the ensuing overseas debt meant that existing government approaches could not be sustained. In a short period of time New Zealand was transformed from a highly regulated, highly protected, public sector-dominated economy into one of the world's most open and deregulated economies. The policies introduced were designed to:

- Increase flexibility in the labour market.
- Reduce inflation.
- Encourage free trade.

These policies were intended to lower costs, increase exports and so provide ideal conditions for increases in GDP, i.e. *growth*. The private sector, free from unnecessary government control and motivated by profit, would take economic advantage of the situation and *grow*. But the process of change was very painful for many New Zealanders. The negative effects were unemployment and social stress. Nevertheless this economic philosophy continued to dominate government policy for the next decade or so.

In spite of these policies of transformation, New Zealand's growth rates, compared with other OECD countries, have been low.

Today, **improved growth is a target of government policy**.

ISBN: 9780170215718

Economics for NCEA Level 2

Fiscal policy

The term **fiscal** refers to government revenue (taxation) and expenditure (spending). The government's fiscal policy is their intention regarding revenue and expenditure.

Fiscal policy and growth

Government policies designed to improve growth may include:

Government spending on education

Increased spending in these areas:

- Curriculum review: Making subjects more applicable to the needs of employers.
- Assessment review: Introduction of NCEA and acknowledging a greater range of skills.
- Subsidised work schemes and training.
- Introduction of National Standards.

All of which are designed to increase labour productivity.

Government spending on investment in infrastructure

Providing a suitable environment for businesses to perform and grow. For example, increased spending to improve Auckland's traffic congestion – the Victoria Park Tunnel, the Western Ring Road and improved public transport.

Taxation

The other part of fiscal policy is taxation. While increased taxation allows greater government spending on growth issues, it is a cost to producers and thus acts as a brake on their efforts to grow. The company tax rate and top personal tax rate were reduced by the National Government in 2010.

ISBN: 9780170215718

ISBN: 9780170215718

ACTIVITY

Rugby World Cup: Queens Wharf project leader up on Cloud 9

Aug 22, 2011

... He said commentators questioning the estimated $700 million direct economic return from the Cup were overly pessimistic.

New Zealand has already benefited through the accelerated upgrade of infrastructure like stadiums, roads and public transport, tourism facilities and investments in hotels and restaurants.

"Many of the projects such as the upgrade to transport and hospitality facilities would likely have never happened or been delayed for years."

He was confident businesses would build new relationships that would help them win exports after the Cup.

a Fully explain how government funding of the Rugby World Cup 2011 could impact on growth.

b Use the AS/AD model to illustrate your answer.

aggregate demand (AD): total demand from all sectors of the economy
aggregate supply (AS): total supply
appreciation: a rise in the value of the dollar in a floating exchange rate
AS/AD model: macroeconomic model showing the relationship between aggregate demand and aggregate supply

Balance of Payments: a record of New Zealand's transactions with the rest of the world
business cycle: the pattern of growth in an economy over time

capital: man-made resources
Capital Account: one of three accounts making up the Balance of Payments
census: a Statistics New Zealand survey of entire population
circular flow model: macroeconomic model showing interdependence of sectors within an economy
Consumer Price Index (CPI): statistical index showing changes in prices of products bought by an average household
cost-push inflation: a rise in the general level of prices caused by decreases in aggregate supply
Current Account: one of three accounts making up the Balance of Payments
customs union: a type of free trade area that has free trade between members

and common barriers to trade with the rest of the world

cyclical unemployment: a form of unemployment caused by changes in the business cycle

deflation: decreases in the general level of prices
demand for labour: the available number of jobs at each wage rate
demand-pull inflation: inflation caused by increases in aggregate demand
dependence: one-way reliance
depreciation: a fall in the value of the dollar in a floating exchange rate
derived demand: the demand for a factor of production
disinflation: a special type of inflation where there is a fall or slowing in the rate of inflation

employment: utilisation of resources in the labour market
Employment Relations Act (ERA): legislation providing the framework for employment
entrepreneur: the decision-maker and risk-taker
exchange rate: the value of one currency expressed in relation to another currency
expenditure method: a method of calculating GDP using aggregate demand
export: goods and services sold overseas
export receipts: the financial flow into the circular flow associated with exports
export subsidy: a form of trade protection that assists exporters by paying some costs of production and producing lower-priced goods that are more competitive overseas

factor endowments: resources of an economy
final demand: demand for a good or service
Financial Account: one of three accounts making up the Balance of Payments
financial sector: a sector of the circular flow representing the financial flows of savings and investment
firms sector: a sector of the circular flow representing the financial flow of investment
fiscal drag: the effect of progressive tax rates on rising incomes
fiscal policy: governmental decisions regarding tax revenue and expenditure
free trade: trade without artificial barriers
Free Trade Agreements (FTA): agreements between member nations to have no artificial barriers to trade
free trade areas: a type of free trade area that has free trade between members and each member has its own barriers to trade with the rest of the world
frictional unemployment: a type of unemployment caused by workers moving between jobs

ISBN: 9780170215718

geographical mobility: the ability of a resource to move from one location to another

government sector: a sector of the circular flow that represents central and local government

Gross Domestic Product (GDP): the value of goods and services produced in an economy in one year measured at market prices

growth: increases in real output

Household Labour Force Survey (HLFS): a Statistics New Zealand survey of employment and unemployment

household sector: a sector of the circular flow representing consumers

human resources: a factor of production including all effort by people, including both labour and the entrepreneur

import: goods and services bought overseas

import payments: financial flow associated with imports

import quota: a form of trade protection that limits the number of a good that can be imported

income: payments for resources, flow from firms to households

Income Method: a method of calculating GDP using payments for resources

independence: no reliance

indexation: where incomes are tied to the CPI, ensuring adjustments for inflation are made to maintain living standards

inflation: a persistent rise in the general level of prices

injections: flows into the circular flow

intangible commodities: services

interdependence: mutual (two-way) reliance

interest: a payment made for capital (specific economic term), also refers to the cost of borrowing finance

investment: increase in man-made resources

involuntary unemployed: willing to work at the wage rate but unable to find work

labour: a factor of production including all effort by people excluding entrepreneur

labour market: where the factor of production of labour is bought and sold

land: natural resources

ISBN: 9780170215718

macroeconomic model: an economic system that demonstrates how the entire economy operates instead of individual markets within the economy

man-made resources: capital

minimum wage: a legal limit on the lowest level of wages able to be paid

monetary policy: government decisions regarding the money supply, implemented in New Zealand by the Reserve Bank (RBNZ)

money flows: financial flows

natural rate of unemployment: a persistent minimum of unemployment that cannot be removed

natural resources: a factor of production provided by nature

Net Social Welfare: a measure of growth that includes non-economic factors

nominal wage rate: the dollar value of a wage

occupational mobility: the ability of a resource to move from one production process to another

Official Cash Rate (OCR): an interest rate set by the Reserve Bank to implement monetary policy and maintain price stability

offshore services: exported services consumed overseas

onshore services: exported services consumed within New Zealand

operating balance: taxation less government spending (including transfer payments but excluding government spending on capital items)

opportunity cost: next best alternative foregone

overseas sector: a sector of the circular flow that represents the rest of the world

Policy Targets Agreement (PTA): agreement between government and RBNZ outlining acceptable inflation target

pollution: negative environmental impact of production

price freezes: making the increase of prices illegal

price level: the general level of prices, a measure of aggregated prices

price-taker: an economy unable to have an impact on world prices

Production Method: a method of calculating GDP using the value added at each stage of production

Production Possibility Frontier (PPF): a model of the maximum level of production possible with given resources or technology

productive capacity: a measure of an economy's ability to produce

ISBN: 9780170215718

productivity: output per unit of input
profit: return paid to the entrepreneur
progressive tax system: a tax regime that increases the tax rate as incomes rise
protection: artificial barriers to trade
purchasing power of money: a measure of the ability of incomes to buy goods or services

Quantity Theory of Money: an economic model demonstrating the relationship between money supply and the price level
Quarterly Employment Survey (QES): a Statistics New Zealand survey of employment

real flows: flows of goods and services and of resources in the economy
real GDP: GDP adjusted for the impact of rises in the general price level
real GDP per capita: real GDP adjusted for population size
real income: real output
real wage rate: the nominal wage rate adjusted for inflation or the purchasing power of wages
rent: return on natural resources
resource depletion: a negative impact of growth where resources are not used in a sustainable manner and lost through over-use
Resource Management Act (RMA): legislation providing the framework for resource use
return: the income paid to a resource for using it in production
rules and regulations: a trade barrier using 'red tape' to slow or hamper trade

savings: consumption now forgone
seasonal unemployment: a type of frictional unemployment affected by the changing season
sticky wages: a nominal wage rate's inability to move downward resulting in disequilibrium in the labour market
structural unemployment: a type of unemployment caused by a mismatch between workers' skills and the skills required by employers
subsidies: a payment from government to producers to help pay costs of production
supply of labour: the number of workers available at a range of wage rates
supply side policies: policies designed to make business easier, such as deregulation

ISBN: 9780170215718

tangible commodities: goods
tariff: a tax on imports
taxes: a payment to government paid on revenue or expenditure
Terms of Trade (TOT) Index: a ratio of import prices over export prices
Trade Weighted Index (TWI): an average measure of a currency's value over several other significant currencies
transfer payment: a one-way payment from the government

underemployment: a measure of workers working below their skill level or for less time that desired
unemployment: labour force willing and able to work but unable to find a job

voluntary unemployed: workers who are not willing to work at the current wage

wage: a payment for labour
weighted: giving more importance or significance to some factors over others
withdrawal: a financial flow out of the circular flow
world price: price of goods and services traded internationally

ISBN: 9780170215718

Index

ISBN: 9780170215718

ISBN: 9780170215718